UNLOCK

Second Edition

2

Listening, Speaking & Critical Thinking

STUDENT'S BOOK WITH DIGITAL PACK

Stephanie Dimond-Bayir and Kimberly Russell
with Chris Sowton, Jennifer Farmer
and Carolyn Flores

CAMBRIDGE
UNIVERSITY PRESS

CAMBRIDGE
UNIVERSITY PRESS & ASSESSMENT

Shaftesbury Road, Cambridge CB2 8EA, United Kingdom

One Liberty Plaza, 20th Floor, New York, NY 10006, USA

477 Williamstown Road, Port Melbourne, VIC 3207, Australia

314–321, 3rd Floor, Plot 3, Splendor Forum, Jasola District Centre, New Delhi – 110025, India

103 Penang Road, #05–06/07, Visioncrest Commercial, Singapore 238467

Cambridge University Press & Assessment is a department of the University of Cambridge.

We share the University's mission to contribute to society through the pursuit of education, learning and research at the highest international levels of excellence.

www.cambridge.org
Information on this title: www.cambridge.org/9781009031462

First published 2014
Second Edition 2019
Second Edition update published 2021

20 19 18 17 16 15 14 13

Printed in Malaysia by Vivar Printing

A catalogue record for this publication is available from the British Library

ISBN 978-1-009-03146-2 Listening, Speaking and Critical Thinking Student's Book with Digital Pack 2
ISBN 978-1-009-03134-9 Listening, Speaking and Critical Thinking Student's eBook with Digital Pack 2

CONTENTS

MAP OF THE BOOK

UNIT	VIDEO	LISTENING	VOCABULARY
1 PLACES Listening 1: A podcast about homes around the world (Geography) Listening 2: A profile of Stanley Park in Vancouver, Canada (Urban planning)	The Grand Canal	***Key skills:*** Predicting content using visuals Distinguishing fact from opinion ***Additional skills:*** Understanding key vocabulary Listening for main ideas Taking notes on detail Listening for opinion Synthesizing ***Pronunciation for listening:*** Vowel sounds /eɪ/, /ɒ/, /ɪ/, /ʌ/	Descriptive adjectives
2 FESTIVALS AND CELEBRATIONS Listening 1: Interviews about three cultural festivals (Social sciences) Listening 2: A discussion about Thanksgiving in the US and Canada (Cultural studies)	Harbin's ice festival	***Key skills:*** Taking notes Listening for main ideas ***Additional skills:*** Understanding key vocabulary Predicting content using visuals Listening for detail Recognizing examples Synthesizing ***Pronunciation for listening:*** Sentence stress	Collocations with *go to, take* and *have*
3 THE INTERNET AND TECHNOLOGY Listening 1: A student radio programme about developments in robotics (Sociology) Listening 2: A news report about how computers affect memory (Psychology)	Fibre optic cables	***Key skill:*** Listening for reasons ***Additional skills:*** Understanding key vocabulary Using your knowledge Taking notes on main ideas Listening for detail Synthesizing ***Pronunciation for listening:*** Consonant sounds /s/, /ʃ/, /ʧ/ Strong /æ/ and weak /ə/	Vocabulary for technology
4 WEATHER AND CLIMATE Listening 1: A student discussion on how weather affects people's moods (Psychology and Social sciences) Listening 2: A news report on global warming and its effects on rainforests (Geography, Environmental science)	The impact of oceans on climate	***Key skill:*** Predicting ideas from research ***Additional skills:*** Understanding key vocabulary Using your knowledge Predicting content using visuals Taking notes on main ideas Listening for detail Synthesizing ***Pronunciation for listening:*** Rising and falling intonation to understand mood Vowel sounds /ɒ/ and /əʊ/	Verb collocations

	GRAMMAR	CRITICAL THINKING	SPEAKING
	Review of the past simple	Deciding if ideas are relevant	*Speaking skills:* Signposting an opinion Organizing information for a presentation *Pronunciation for speaking:* Connecting speech *Speaking task:* Give a presentation about an interesting place
	Review of present tense question forms The present continuous	Creating a persuasive argument	*Speaking skills:* Making suggestions Agreeing and disagreeing *Speaking task:* Choose an event from a festival and persuade your group to go to it
	can / be able to	Evaluating advantages and disadvantages	*Speaking skills:* Giving additional and contrasting information Giving a spoken report *Speaking task:* Present a report about a device or technology
	Gerunds and infinitives Future forms • Decisions and plans (*will, be going to,* present continuous) • Predictions (*will, be going to*)	Evaluating effects	*Speaking skill:* Linking words to explain cause and effect *Speaking task:* Give a presentation about climate change

UNIT	VIDEO	LISTENING	VOCABULARY
5 SPORTS AND COMPETITION Listening 1: A student presentation on unusual sports (Sports science) Listening 2: A discussion about money in sport (Sports science)	Kasparov versus Deep Blue	*Key skills:* Listening for bias Supporting opinions *Additional skills:* Understanding key vocabulary Listening for main ideas Taking notes Synthesizing *Pronunciation for listening:* Making corrections	Vocabulary for sport and competition (e.g. *competition, score, prize, fan, champion, compete)*
6 BUSINESS Listening 1: A conversation between a business student and a professor about a project (Business studies) Listening 2: A conversation between a business owner and a consultant (Business, Marketing)	Food in coffee shops	*Key skill:* Listening for numbers *Additional skills:* Understanding key vocabulary Using your knowledge Taking notes on detail Listening for reaction Making inferences Synthesizing *Pronunciation for listening:* Pronouncing numbers	Phrasal verbs
7 PEOPLE Listening 1: A student presentation on creative people (History) Listening 2: A student conversation about a project (Business studies, Industrial design)	Trash artists	*Key skill:* Listening for attitude *Additional skills:* Understanding key vocabulary Using your knowledge Listening for main ideas Taking notes on detail Synthesizing *Pronunciation for listening:* Intonation for emotion and interest	Adjective endings *-ed* and *-ing*
8 THE UNIVERSE Listening 1: A radio programme about space travel (Space studies) Listening 2: A discussion on funding for space exploration (Space studies)	Empire of the sun	*Key skill:* Understanding meaning from context *Additional skills:* Understanding key vocabulary Predicting content using visuals Listening to an introduction Taking notes on detail Listening for main ideas Synthesizing *Pronunciation for listening:* Words with easily-confused sounds	Vocabulary for problems and solutions

GRAMMAR	CRITICAL THINKING	SPEAKING
Conditionals • The zero conditional and the first conditional Adverbs of degree	Building a strong argument	***Speaking skills:*** Emphasizing a point Asking for and giving clarification ***Speaking task:*** Have a discussion about money in sport.
Comparatives and superlatives	Identify solutions to problems	***Speaking skill:*** Giving advice ***Speaking task:*** Give advice to a failing business
The past continuous • Forming the past continuous • The past continuous and the past simple	Evaluate the importance of information	***Speaking skills:*** Time order Examples and details ***Speaking task:*** Give a presentation about a remarkable person and his or her work
The second conditional	Finding the best solution to a problem	***Speaking skills:*** Turn-taking Showing levels of agreement ***Speaking task:*** Discuss how to get children interested in space exploration

YOUR GUIDE TO UNLOCK

Unlock your academic potential

Unlock Second Edition is a six-level, academic-light English course created to build the skills and language students need for their studies (CEFR Pre-A1 to C1). It develops students' ability to think critically in an academic context right from the start of their language learning. Every level has 100% new inspiring video on a range of academic topics.

Confidence in teaching.
Joy in learning.

Better Learning WITH UNLOCK SECOND EDITION

Better Learning is our simple approach where insights we've gained from research have helped shape content that drives results. We've listened to teachers all around the world and made changes so that *Unlock* Second Edition better supports students along the way to academic success.

CRITICAL THINKING

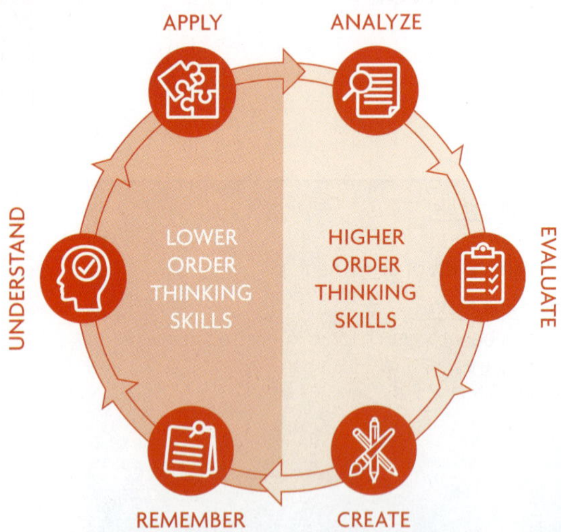

Critical thinking in *Unlock* Second Edition ...

- is **informed** by a range of academic research from Bloom in the 1950s, to Krathwohl and Anderson in the 2000s, to more recent considerations relating to 21st Century Skills
- has a **refined** syllabus with a better mix of higher- and lower-order critical thinking skills
- is **measurable**, with objectives and self-evaluation so students can track their critical thinking progress
- is **transparent** so teachers and students know when and why they're developing critical thinking skills
- is **supported** with professional development material for teachers so teachers can teach with confidence

... so that students have the best possible chance of academic success.

INSIGHT

Most classroom time is currently spent on developing lower-order critical thinking skills. Students need to be able to use higher-order critical thinking skills too.

CONTENT

Unlock Second Edition includes the right mix of lower- and higher-order thinking skills development in every unit, with clear learning objectives.

RESULTS

Students are better prepared for their academic studies and have the confidence to apply the critical thinking skills they have developed.

DIGITAL CLASSROOM MATERIAL

The *Unlock* Second Edition Digital Classroom Material ...

- offers extra, **motivating** practice in speaking, critical thinking and language
- provides a **convenient** bank of language and skills reference informed by our exclusive Corpus research
- is easily **accessible** and **navigable** from students' mobile phones
- is fully **integrated** into every unit
- provides Unlock-**specific** activities to extend the lesson whenever you see this symbol

... so that students can easily get the right, extra practice they need, when they need it.

INSIGHT

The digital classroom material is most effective when it's an integral, well-timed part of a lesson.

CONTENT

Every unit of *Unlock* Second Edition is enhanced with bespoke digital classroom material to extend the skills and language students are learning in the book. The symbol shows when to use the material.

RESULTS

Students are motivated by having relevant extension material on their mobile phones to maximize their language learning. Teachers are reassured that the material adds real language-learning value to their lessons.

RESEARCH

We have gained deeper insights to inform *Unlock* Second Edition by ...

- carrying out **extensive market research** with teachers and students to fully understand their needs throughout the course's development
- consulting **academic research** into critical thinking
- refining our vocabulary syllabus using our **exclusive Corpus research**

... so that you can be assured of the quality of *Unlock* Second Edition.

INSIGHT

- Consultation with global Advisory Panel
- Comprehensive reviews of material
- Face-to-face interviews and Skype™ calls
- Classroom observations

CONTENT

- Improved critical thinking
- 100% new video and video lessons
- Clearer contexts for language presentation and practice
- Text-by-text glossaries
- Digital workbook with more robust content
- Comprehensive teacher support

RESULTS

"Thank you for all the effort you've put into developing Unlock *Second Edition. As far as I can see, I think the new edition is more academic and more appealing to young adults."*

Burçin Gönülsen,
Işık Üniversity, Turkey

HOW *UNLOCK* WORKS

Unlock your knowledge

Encourages discussion around the themes of the unit with inspiration from interesting questions and striking images.

UNLOCK YOUR KNOWLEDGE

Work with a partner. Look at the photo and answer the questions.

1 What is the machine in the photo? What does it do?
2 What types of things can we learn from studying the night sky?
3 Huge amounts of money are spent on studying space and space exploration. Do you think we should spend so much money on this research? Why / Why not?

Watch and listen

Features an engaging and motivating video which generates interest in the topic and develops listening skills.

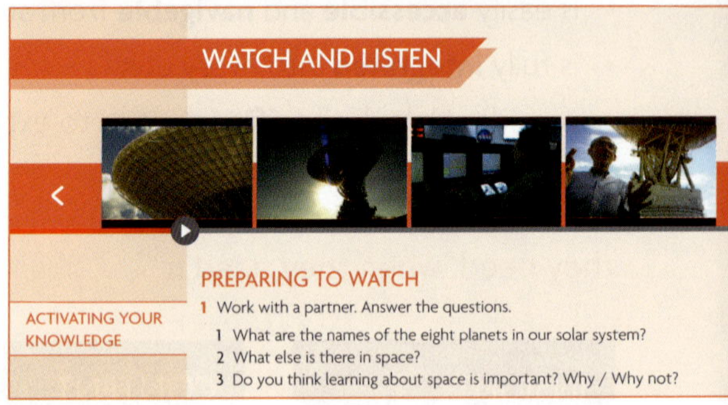

WATCH AND LISTEN

ACTIVATING YOUR KNOWLEDGE

PREPARING TO WATCH

1 Work with a partner. Answer the questions.
1 What are the names of the eight planets in our solar system?
2 What else is there in space?
3 Do you think learning about space is important? Why / Why not?

LISTENING

Listening 1

Provides information about the topic and practises pre-listening, while-listening and post-listening skills. This section may also include a focus on pronunciation which will further enhance listening comprehension.

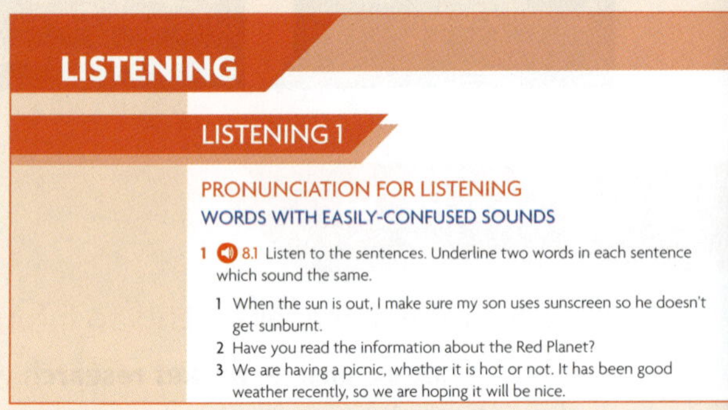

LISTENING

LISTENING 1

PRONUNCIATION FOR LISTENING

WORDS WITH EASILY-CONFUSED SOUNDS

1 8.1 Listen to the sentences. Underline two words in each sentence which sound the same.
1 When the sun is out, I make sure my son uses sunscreen so he doesn't get sunburnt.
2 Have you read the information about the Red Planet?
3 We are having a picnic, whether it is hot or not. It has been good weather recently, so we are hoping it will be nice.

Language development

Practises the vocabulary and grammar from Listening 1 and pre-teaches the vocabulary and grammar for Listening 2.

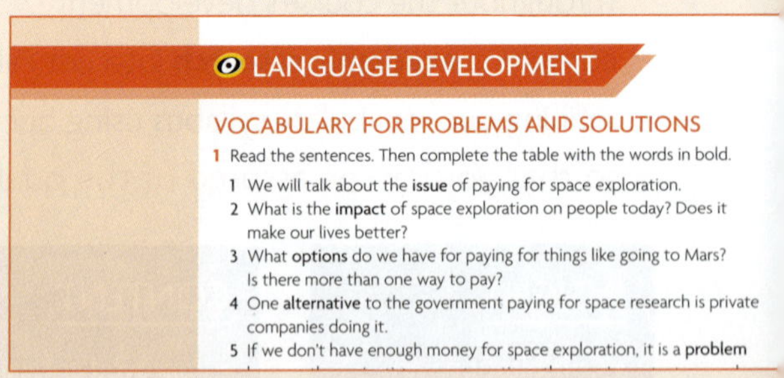

LANGUAGE DEVELOPMENT

VOCABULARY FOR PROBLEMS AND SOLUTIONS

1 Read the sentences. Then complete the table with the words in bold.
1 We will talk about the **issue** of paying for space exploration.
2 What is the **impact** of space exploration on people today? Does it make our lives better?
3 What **options** do we have for paying for things like going to Mars? Is there more than one way to pay?
4 One **alternative** to the government paying for space research is private companies doing it.
5 If we don't have enough money for space exploration, it is a **problem**

Listening 2

Presents a second listening text on the topic, often in a different format, and serves as a model for the speaking task.

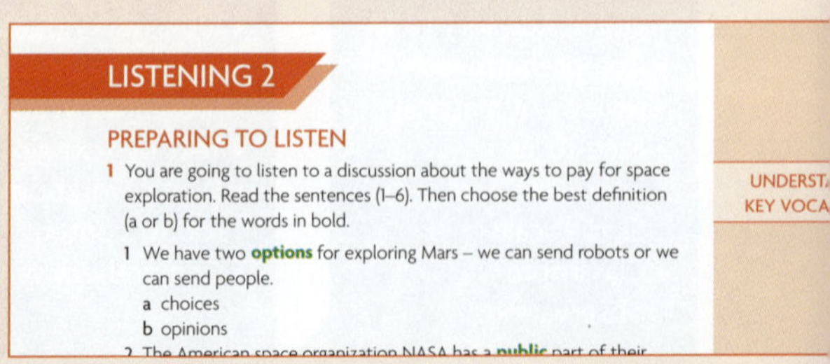

LISTENING 2

PREPARING TO LISTEN

1 You are going to listen to a discussion about the ways to pay for space exploration. Read the sentences (1–6). Then choose the best definition (a or b) for the words in bold.
1 We have two **options** for exploring Mars – we can send robots or we can send people.
a choices
b opinions

SPEAKING

Critical thinking

Develops the lower- and higher-order thinking skills required for the speaking task.

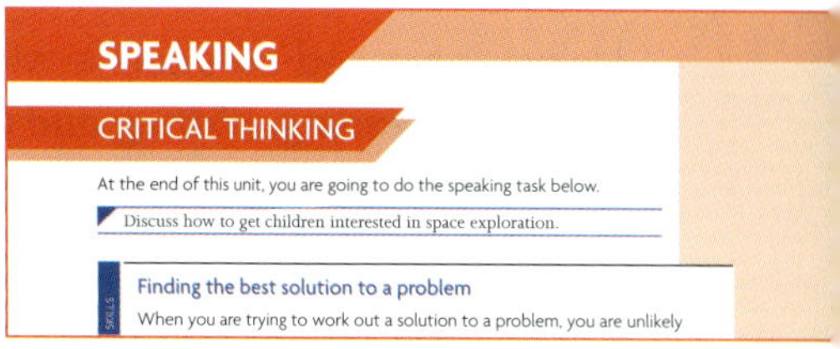

SPEAKING

CRITICAL THINKING

At the end of this unit, you are going to do the speaking task below.

Discuss how to get children interested in space exploration.

Finding the best solution to a problem

When you are trying to work out a solution to a problem, you are unlikely

Preparation for speaking

Presents and practises functional language, pronunciation and speaking strategies for the speaking task.

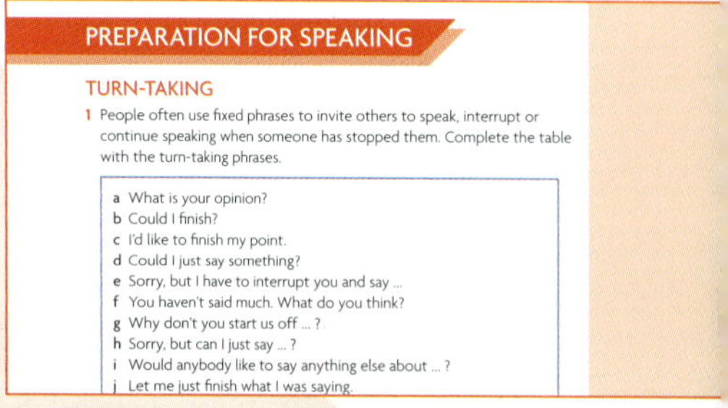

PREPARATION FOR SPEAKING

TURN-TAKING

1 People often use fixed phrases to invite others to speak, interrupt or continue speaking when someone has stopped them. Complete the table with the turn-taking phrases.

a What is your opinion?
b Could I finish?
c I'd like to finish my point.
d Could I just say something?
e Sorry, but I have to interrupt you and say ...
f You haven't said much. What do you think?
g Why don't you start us off ... ?
h Sorry, but can I just say ... ?
i Would anybody like to say anything else about ... ?
j Let me just finish what I was saying.

Speaking task

Uses the skills and language learned throughout the unit to support students in producing a presentational or interactional speaking task. This is the unit's main learning objective.

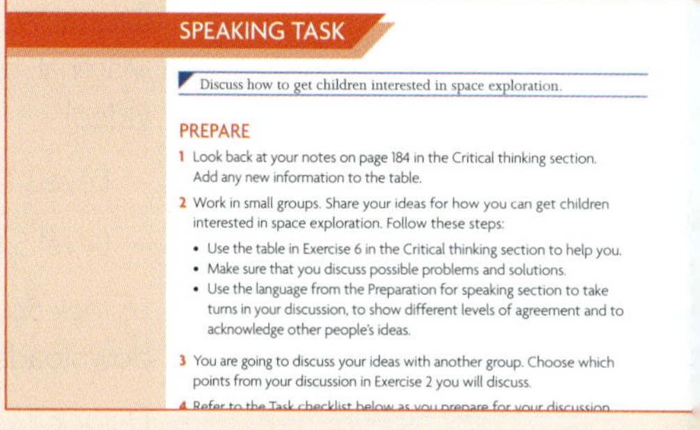

SPEAKING TASK

Discuss how to get children interested in space exploration.

PREPARE

1 Look back at your notes on page 184 in the Critical thinking section. Add any new information to the table.

2 Work in small groups. Share your ideas for how you can get children interested in space exploration. Follow these steps:
- Use the table in Exercise 6 in the Critical thinking section to help you.
- Make sure that you discuss possible problems and solutions.
- Use the language from the Preparation for speaking section to take turns in your discussion, to show different levels of agreement and to acknowledge other people's ideas.

3 You are going to discuss your ideas with another group. Choose which points from your discussion in Exercise 2 you will discuss.

4 Refer to the Task checklist below as you prepare for your discussion.

Objectives review

Allows learners to evaluate how well they have mastered the skills covered in the unit.

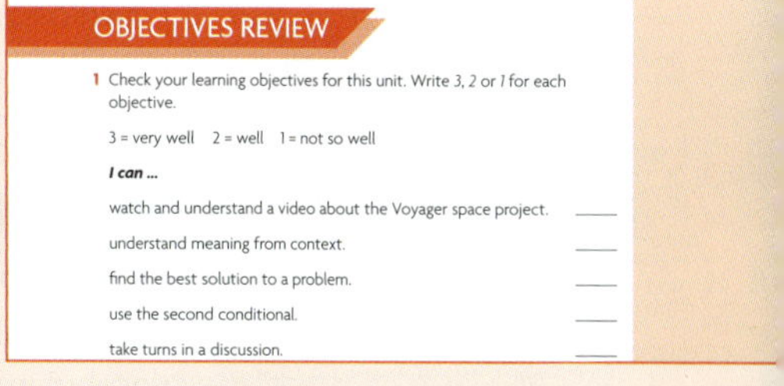

OBJECTIVES REVIEW

1 Check your learning objectives for this unit. Write 3, 2 or 1 for each objective.

3 = very well 2 = well 1 = not so well

I can ...

watch and understand a video about the Voyager space project. ___
understand meaning from context. ___
find the best solution to a problem. ___
use the second conditional. ___
take turns in a discussion. ___

Wordlist

Lists the key vocabulary from the unit. The most frequent words used at this level in an academic context are highlighted. ⊙

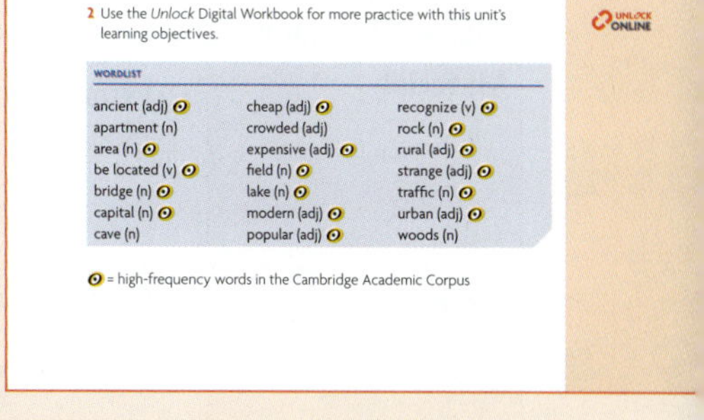

2 Use the *Unlock* Digital Workbook for more practice with this unit's learning objectives.

UNLOCK ONLINE

WORDLIST

ancient (adj) ⊙	cheap (adj) ⊙	recognize (v) ⊙
apartment (n)	crowded (adj)	rock (n) ⊙
area (n) ⊙	expensive (adj) ⊙	rural (adj) ⊙
be located (v) ⊙	field (n) ⊙	strange (adj) ⊙
bridge (n) ⊙	lake (n) ⊙	traffic (n) ⊙
capital (n) ⊙	modern (adj) ⊙	urban (adj) ⊙
cave (n)	popular (adj) ⊙	woods (n)

⊙ = high-frequency words in the Cambridge Academic Corpus

COMPONENTS

Unlock offers 56 hours per Student's Book, which is extendable to 90 hours with the Digital Pack, and other additional activities in the Teacher's Manual and Development Pack.

Unlock is a paired-skills course with two separate Student's Books per level. For levels 1–5 (CEFR A1 – C1), these are ***Reading, Writing and Critical Thinking*** and ***Listening, Speaking and Critical Thinking***. They share the same unit topics so you have access to a wide range of material at each level. Each Student's Book provides access to the Digital Pack.

Unlock Basic has been developed for pre-A1 learners. ***Unlock Basic Skills*** integrates reading, writing, listening, speaking and critical thinking in one book to provide students with an effective and manageable learning experience. ***Unlock Basic Literacy*** develops and builds confidence in literacy. The *Basic* books also share the same unit topics and so can be used together or separately, and ***Unlock Basic Literacy*** can be used for self-study.

Student components

Resource	Description	Access
Student's Books	• Levels 1–5 come with the Digital Pack (Digital Workbook, Digital Classroom Material, downloadable audio and video) – Levels 1–4 (8 units) – Level 5 (10 units) • *Unlock Basic Skills* comes with downloadable audio and video (11 units) • *Unlock Basic Literacy* comes with downloadable audio (11 units)	• The Digital Pack (Digital Workbook, Digital Classroom Material, downloadable audio and video) is accessed on our **learning platform** via the unique code inside the front cover of the Student's Book • The audio and video are downloadable from the Student's Resources section on the **learning platform**
Digital Workbook	• Levels 1–5 only • Extension activities to further practise the language and skills learned • All-new vocabulary activities in the Digital Workbook practise the target vocabulary in new contexts	• The Digital Workbook is on our **learning platform** and is accessed via the unique code inside the front cover of the Student's Book
Digital Classroom Material	• Levels 1–5 only • Extra practice in speaking, critical thinking and language	• Please go to **cambridgeone.org** to access the digital classroom material. • Students use the same login details as for the **learning platform**, and then they are logged in for a year
Video	• Levels 1–5 and *Unlock Basic Skills* only • All the video from the course	• The video is downloadable from the Student's Resources section on the **learning platform**
Audio	• All the audio from the course	• The audio is downloadable from the Student's Resources section on the **learning platform**

Teacher components

Resource	Description	Access
Teacher's Manual and Development Pack	• One manual covers Levels 1–5 • It contains flexible lesson plans, lesson objectives, additional activities and common learner errors as well as professional development for teachers, *Developing critical thinking skills in your students* • It comes with downloadable audio and video, vocabulary worksheets and peer-to-peer teacher training worksheets	• The audio, video and worksheets are downloadable from the Teacher Resources section on the **learning platform**
Presentation Plus	• Software for interactive whiteboards so you can present the pages of the Student's Books and easily play audio and video, and check answers	• Presentation Plus is available from the Teacher Resources section on our **learning platform**

LEARNING OBJECTIVES	IN THIS UNIT YOU WILL ...
Watch and listen	watch and understand a video about the Grand Canal in Venice.
Listening skills	predict content using visuals; distinguish fact from opinion.
Critical thinking	decide if ideas are relevant.
Grammar	use past simple statements and questions.
Speaking skills	signpost an opinion; organize information for a presentation.
Speaking task	give a presentation about an interesting place.

UNIT 1

PLACES

UNLOCK YOUR KNOWLEDGE

Work with a partner. Look at the photo and answer the questions.

1 Do you think the houses in the photo are unusual? Why?
2 Why do people choose to live in unusual homes?
3 Would you prefer to live in a house or an apartment building? Why?
4 What are some of the advantages of living near the sea? On a mountain? In a city centre?

PLUS

WATCH AND LISTEN

PREPARING TO WATCH

ACTIVATING YOUR KNOWLEDGE

1 Work with a partner. Answer the questions.

1 Where is the city of Venice?
2 What do you know about Venice?
3 Why do tourists like to visit old towns or cities like Venice?

PREDICTING CONTENT USING VISUALS

2 You are going to watch a video about Venice. Look at the photos from the video. Work with a partner. Discuss how this city looks different from other cities.

GLOSSARY

canal (n) a river made by people
gondola (n) a narrow boat with a raised point at both ends, used on canals in Venice
man-made (adj) not natural, but made by people
palace (n) a large, important house or building, often where a king or queen lives
stilts (n) long pieces of wood or metal that a building stands on so that it is above the ground or water

WHILE WATCHING

UNDERSTANDING MAIN IDEAS

3 Watch the video. Write *T* (true) or *F* (false) next to the statements. Then correct the false statements.

_____ 1 There are a lot of canals and bridges.
_____ 2 Most of the islands between the canals are big.
_____ 3 Today, Venice is important for art and businesses.
_____ 4 People know Venice as a popular tourist centre.
_____ 5 The Grand Canal is the smallest canal in Venice.
_____ 6 The Grand Canal is a man-made river.
_____ 7 Another name for Venice is 'The City of Boats'.

UNDERSTANDING DETAIL

4 Watch again. Answer the questions.

1 What does Venice have instead of busy roads?
2 What don't you see on them?
3 What is the name of the special boats in the video?
4 What are palaces and other buildings in Venice built on?
5 What was the Ca' d'Oro palace decorated with?
6 What is the Rialto Bridge made of?

5 Work with a partner. Complete each sentence with a number from the box.

30	two	15	117	300	400

1 There are ________ islands between the canals and ________ bridges in Venice.
2 The Grand Canal is more than ________ miles long.
3 For nearly ________ years, you could only cross the Grand Canal on the Rialto Bridge.
4 A gondola ride usually takes ________ minutes.
5 The palace was built in the ________th century.

MAKING INFERENCES

6 Work with a partner. The speaker in the video says that a gondola ride is 'one of the best 30 minutes you can spend in your life'.

1 Why do you think the speaker says this?
2 Do you agree with his opinion? Why / Why not?

DISCUSSION

7 Work in a small group. Discuss the questions.

1 What do you think it is like to live in Venice?
2 Does your hometown or country have any interesting canals, rivers or roads?

8 Look at the advert for gondola boat rides and answer the questions.

1 Can you take a boat ride on Monday night?
2 Is there a boat ride at 10.00 in the morning?
3 Where does the boat ride begin?
4 How much does it cost?
5 Why do you think the boat rides are from April until October?
6 Why do the boats have life jackets?

Gondola Boat Rides

Starting at the Ca' d'Oro
Every day of the week
11.00 am, 2.00 pm, 3.00 pm

€20 per person

from April to October

We have life jackets for everyone!

LISTENING

LISTENING 1

PREPARING TO LISTEN

UNDERSTANDING KEY VOCABULARY

1 Read the sentences (1–8). Then write the correct form of the words in bold next to the definitions (a–h).

1 Look at the pictures. Do you **recognize** any of the places? Where are they?
2 Some of these places are very **strange**. They are not like other places.
3 The **capital** of the United Kingdom is London. The Prime Minister lives there.
4 These **ancient** buildings are more than 1,000 years old.
5 Mountains have a lot of **rocks** on them. They make it difficult to walk.
6 Kara lives in a small **apartment** in Tokyo. It's in a big building.
7 We have to drive over the **bridge** to get to the island.
8 Lisa found a large **cave** in the mountain. It was very dark and cold inside.

a ________ (adj) different from the usual or normal; unusual or not expected
b ________ (n) something built over a river or road that lets people, cars or trains go across
c ________ (n) a hard piece of the material that the Earth is made of
d ________ (v) to know something because you have seen it before
e ________ (n) a large hole in the side of a mountain or under the ground
f ________ (adj) from a long time ago; very old
g ________ (n) a room or set of rooms in a building for someone to live in
h ________ (n) the most important city in a country or state, where the government is

SKILLS

Predicting content using visuals

Before you listen, look quickly at the photos related to the listening. Think of important or 'key' words to talk about the photos. Think about the size, shape or place of things in each photo. This helps you understand more about the topic when you listen.

2 You are going to listen to a podcast about homes around the world. Look at the photos. What do you think you will learn about homes?

3 Work with a partner. Look at the photos. Match the words from the box to the photos. In some items, more than one answer is possible.

PREDICTING CONTENT USING VISUALS

an-cient	bridge	cave	rock	strange

a

____

b

____

c

____

d

____

PRONUNCIATION FOR LISTENING

SKILLS

Vowel sounds /eɪ/, /ɒ/, /ɪ/, /ʌ/

Pronunciation is just as important for listening as it is for speaking. When you improve your English pronunciation, you also improve your ability to understand others when you are listening.

1.1 Listen to each of the words below. Notice the different vowel sounds in each word.

/eɪ/ place   /ɒ/ hot   /ɪ/ quick   /ʌ/ up

4 Work with a partner. Say the words from the table below and notice the underlined sound. Write the words from Exercise 3 in the table.

/eɪ/	/ɒ/	/ɪ/	/ʌ/
place	hot	quick	up

5 Write the words from the box below in the table in Exercise 4.

built   hun-dreds   long   say   un-der

6 Work with a partner. Take turns reading aloud different words from the lists below. Your partner should listen carefully and tell you which word you said.

Student A: Cut.
Student B: You said 'cut'. Number 2. List D.

	A	B	C	D
1	hate	hot	hit	hut
2	Kate	cot	kit	cut

WHILE LISTENING

LISTENING FOR MAIN IDEAS

7 1.2 Look at the questions (1–2). Listen to the podcast and circle the correct answers (a–c).

1 The speakers on the podcast are
  a scientists.
  b professors.
  c world travellers.

2 The main topic of the podcast is
  a travelling to different countries.
  b unusual places where people live.
  c a history of ancient houses.

TAKING NOTES ON DETAIL

8 1.2 Listen to the podcast again and complete the student's notes. Then compare your notes with a partner.

- Matmata is in (1)________________ .
  Matmata facts: (2)________________ years old.
  (3)________________ kilometres south of Tunis.
- Cappadocia is in (4)________________ .
  Cappadocia facts: caves formed about (5)________________ years ago.
- The Ponte Vecchio is in (6)________________ .
  Ponte Vecchio facts: built in (7)________________ .
- Neft Dashlari is in (8)________________ .
  Neft Dashlari facts: bridge is (9)__________ kilometres long.
  (10)________________ people live there.

9 Work with a partner. How are the notes in Exercise 8 useful?

DISCUSSION

10 Discuss the questions below in pairs.

1 If you had to live in one of the places on page 19, which one would it be? Explain your reasons.
2 Why would people like to live in the other places?

LANGUAGE DEVELOPMENT

REVIEW OF THE PAST SIMPLE

GRAMMAR

Past simple statements

Use *the past simple* to talk about events that happened in the past. For regular verbs, add *-ed* to the infinitive. Add *-d* to verbs that end in *-e*. Use the same form for all persons (*I, you, we, they, he, she, it*).

They **filmed** some scenes there. (film → film**ed**)

She **lived** there for 20 years. (live → live**d**)

Irregular verbs do not end in *-ed*. Try to learn the past forms of these verbs.

They **made** them out of rock. (make → **made**)

I **saw** some tall apartment buildings. (see → **saw**)

I **went** to Turkey. (go → **went**)

They **built** the bridge in 1345. (build → **built**)

They **put** houses there. (put → **put**)

For negative statements in the past simple, use *did not* (*didn't*) + infinitive.

They **did not live** in Dubai for a long time.

I **didn't see** much of Seoul.

Be is an irregular verb. The past forms of *be* are *was* / *were*. Use *was* with *I* / *he* / *she* / *it*. Use *were* with *you* / *we* / *they*.

When I **was** younger, I went to Turkey.

They **were** very strange buildings.

For negative statements with *be*, use *was not (wasn't)* or *were not (weren't)*.

Marco **wasn't** in Mexico City last week.

They **weren't** there for a long time.

1 Complete the sentences from Listening 1 below with the past form of the verb in brackets.

1 People __________ (change) them into homes during the Roman period.

2 ... I __________ (go) to Cappadocia in Turkey.

3 So they __________ (make) this one ...

4 There __________ (be) another bridge there before, but an accident __________ (destroy) it.

5 They __________ (decide) that the workers __________ (need) somewhere to live, so they __________ (build) a kind of 'city' above the sea.

6 They __________ (put) houses, libraries, schools and even a cinema there.

7 The caves __________ (form) from rock more than 8,000 years ago.

2 Write the past simple verbs from Exercise 1 in the table.

regular (add *-ed* / *-d*)	irregular
changed	*went*

3 Work with a partner. Choose one of the topics below to discuss.

1 Talk about a home you used to live in.
2 Talk about buildings you saw on your last holiday.

GRAMMAR

Past simple questions

For *Yes* / *No* questions in the past simple, use *Did* + subject + infinitive for all persons (*I*, *you*, *we*, *they*, *he*, *she*, *it*).

Did they build *a new bridge last year?*
Did you live *in Dubai for a long time?*

For information questions, use a *Wh-* word (*Where*, *When*, *Why*, etc.) + *did* + subject + infinitive.

Where did *he* ***go****?*
When did *they* ***build*** *their house?*
Why did *he* ***move*** *to Cairo?*

4 Complete the questions with the words in brackets. Use the past simple.

1 Where ____________________ (you / live) when you were a child?
2 When ____________________ (you / start) living in your home?
3 ____________________ (you / know) the people who lived near you when you were a child?
4 Why ____________________ (you / move) to your home?
5 ____________________ (you / like) the place you lived as a child?

5 Answer the questions in Exercise 4. Write full sentences.

1 ____
2 ____
3 ____
4 ____
5 ____

6 Work with a partner. Ask and answer the questions in Exercise 4.

PLUS

DESCRIPTIVE ADJECTIVES

7 Label the photos with the words from the box. Use the glossary on pages 191–192 to help you.

ancient	cheap	crowded	expensive
modern	popular	rural	urban

a ______________

b ______________

c ______________

d ______________

e ______________

f ______________

g ______________

h ______________

8 Circle the correct words to complete the sentences.

1 The city of Tokyo is a large *rural / urban* area.
2 Many people like to visit Niagara Falls, so we can say that it is a(n) *urban / popular* place to go.
3 Norfolk is a county in England. It has very few cities and a lot of farms. It is one of the most *rural / urban* places in the UK.
4 Hong Kong is a really *cheap / expensive* place to live. The cost of living there is very high.

PLUS

9 Work with a partner. Take turns choosing words from Exercise 7. Give an example of a place or thing for each word. Can your partner guess your words?

Student A: The Great Wall of China is like this.
Student B: Is it 'ancient'?

LISTENING 2

PREPARING TO LISTEN

UNDERSTANDING KEY VOCABULARY

1 Read the sentences (1–8). Then write the words in bold next to the definitions (a–h).

1 I like to live in **urban** places. There are lots of very tall buildings and a lot of fun things to do.
2 In summer, you can swim in a **lake** if you get hot.
3 When I go to the **woods**, I can see many birds and other wild animals.
4 Tokyo is a **modern** city with public transport and a lot of new buildings.
5 What **area** of the city do you live in, the centre or by the park?
6 Paris has a lot of **traffic** because so many people there drive cars every day.
7 A **field** in a park is a nice place to sit and relax because it is very green and sunny.
8 The city of Vancouver **is located** in British Columbia in western Canada.

a ________ (n) open, grassy land
b ________ (n) a part of a larger place
c ________ (adj) relating to the present time and not to the past
d ________ (n) a body of water that has land all around it
e ________ (n) all the cars and trucks using the road
f ________ (adj) belonging to or related to a city
g ________ (n) a place with a lot of trees growing near each other
h ________ (v) to be in a particular place

PLUS

PREDICTING CONTENT USING VISUALS

2 Work with a partner. You are going to listen to a lecture related to the place in the photo below. Choose words from Exercise 1 to describe the photo.

WHILE LISTENING

LISTENING FOR MAIN IDEAS

3 1.3 Listen to the lecture. Check your answers to Exercise 2. What was the lecture about? Circle the correct answer.

a reasons to visit Vancouver, Canada
b the advantages and disadvantages of lots of parks in a city
c different things you can do in Stanley Park

TAKING NOTES ON DETAIL

4 1.3 Listen to the lecture again. According to the speaker, what are the advantages of Stanley Park? What are the disadvantages? Take notes in the table.

advantages	disadvantages
lots of gardens, walking paths, trees and animals	

SKILLS

Distinguishing fact from opinion

A speaker sometimes presents facts (something true) and sometimes opinions (his or her idea about something). Listeners need to think about what they hear. Is there a way to show the information is true? If not, maybe it is an opinion. Signal words and phrases can also help you decide if you hear a fact or an opinion. When the speaker does not use signal words, the context can help you decide.

LISTENING FOR OPINION

5 1.4 Listen and complete the sentences with the signal words and phrases you hear. Are the sentences facts or the speaker's opinions? Write *F* (fact) or *O* (opinion).

1 Obviously , Stanley Park is a large park. F
2 ________ , because it is located in the city of Vancouver, it is the third largest urban park in North America. _____
3 ________ , lots of trees help clean the city air. _____
4 Finally, while ________ these disadvantages might mean that some people would not want to visit Vancouver, ... _____
5 ... ________ that most people would enjoy Vancouver. _____
6 ________ , being close to nature and having a healthy city are worth paying a little more money for. _____

6 Work with a partner. How do you know if the sentences are facts or opinions? Do you agree with the opinions of the speaker?

POST-LISTENING

7 Look at the signal words and phrases for fact and opinion in Exercise 5. Which tense is often used to give facts?

8 The signal words and phrases from Exercise 5 tell you if the information is a general fact or the opinion of the speaker. Add the phrases to the grouping diagrams below.

9 Speakers do not always use signal words to show facts and opinions. Read the sentences from the lecture and write *F* (fact) or *O* (opinion). Check your answers with a partner.

1 Vancouver has the best parts of green forests and city life. ______
2 It has many gardens, walking paths, trees and even animals such as bald eagles, coyotes and seals. ______
3 At the first city meeting, the people of Vancouver asked the national government to give the city 1,000 acres to use as a park. ______
4 It is one of the most beautiful cities in the world. ______

DISCUSSION

SYNTHESIZING

10 Work with a partner. Use ideas from Listening 1 and Listening 2 to answer the following questions.

1 What are some advantages of living in a big city? What are some disadvantages? Is your opinion based on personal experience or other people's experiences? Does it make a difference?
2 Which of the places in Listening 1 and Listening 2 would you most like to live in? Which ones would you only like to visit? Why?

PLUS

SPEAKING

CRITICAL THINKING

At the end of this unit you are going to do the speaking task below.

> Give a presentation about an interesting place. Present factual information and give your opinion about the place you choose.

SKILLS

Deciding if ideas are relevant

Do not try to use all the notes you make when you are looking for information. Some ideas might not be connected to your main idea. Choose information that is connected to the main point of your presentation. This helps listeners to understand and follow your ideas.

EVALUATE

1 Imagine you are going to describe Stanley Park in Vancouver to your class. Read the facts below and choose seven which you think are most connected to the topic.

Facts about Stanley Park in Vancouver, Canada

______ **a** The park is open for fewer hours on a holiday.
______ **b** Stanley Park gets about eight million visitors every year.
______ **c** You can enjoy nature, history, art and many events in the park.
______ **d** The park is named after Lord Frederick Stanley, the Governor General of Canada in 1888.
______ **e** Many kinds of birds live in the park, but some live there only part of the year.
______ **f** The park opened in 1888. It is more than 125 years old.
______ **g** Vancouver takes good care of the park so people can enjoy it for many years.
______ **h** In 1938, the park stopped hiring swimsuits to people at the park.
______ **i** Stanley Park is the third largest urban park in North America. It is 4 km^2.
______ **j** Vancouver spends money to make it easier for everyone to walk and cycle in the park.

2 Compare your answers with a partner. Discuss your reasons for your answers and agree on seven facts.

3 Put the facts 1–7 in order, where 1 is the most relevant to the topic and 7 is the least relevant.

APPLY

4 Choose an interesting place you know. Try to think of a place that other people might not know very well.

5 Find out some facts about the place you chose. Take notes on your own ideas and opinions. Look for an interesting photo of the place.

6 Write an outline for a presentation about the place. Use the table to help you organize your presentation.

plan for presentation	information
1 **introduction and general facts** Name of place? / Country? / Location?	
2 **facts** How old? / Who made it? / Other events?	
3 **opinion (positives)** Interesting? / Beautiful? / Why visit?	
4 **opinion (negatives)** Expensive? / Too crowded? / Problems?	
5 **summary** Good? Go or not?	

EVALUATE

7 Show your table to a partner. Decide if there is any information in the table which is not connected or relevant to the main points of your presentation.

PREPARATION FOR SPEAKING

SIGNPOSTING AN OPINION

SKILLS

When you give your opinion, it is useful to start your sentence with a word or phrase that lets listeners know right away that you are giving your opinion and not stating a fact. It gets them ready to listen for what is coming next. It also helps them think about your opinion and if they agree or not.

I personally feel that most people would enjoy Vancouver.
It seems to me that a lot of people agree with this idea.
In my opinion, being close to nature and having a healthy city are worth paying a little more money for.

1 Work with a partner. Take turns talking about a town or city using the topic suggestions in the box below. Use signal words and phrases and ask follow-up questions.

parks in a town or city   traffic in a town or city
things to do in a town or city

Student A: In my opinion, the traffic is really bad.
Student B: Why is the traffic bad?
Student A: I think it's because a lot of people live there, but there are only a few main roads. They're all really small, too.

ORGANIZING INFORMATION FOR A PRESENTATION

2 When you present information, it is important to organize what you say into different topics so the listener can easily follow your ideas. Match the topics (1–4) to the sentences (a–d).

1 general fact
2 positives
3 negatives
4 summary

a Parks give people places to walk, so they are healthier.
b Having a lot of parks means there is less space to build houses.
c Life in Vancouver has more positives than negatives.
d Europeans came to live in Vancouver in the 1800s.

PLUS

3 1.5 Here is some language that you can use to help your listener understand your ideas. Listen and circle the organizing phrase you hear.

1 *I'd like to talk about / I'd like to tell you about* the city of Vancouver, in British Columbia, Canada.
2 *First of all, / Firstly*, let's look at some of the positives.
3 *I'd also like to talk about / I'd also like to give you* some disadvantages of parks in Vancouver.
4 *In summary, / Finally*, while I think these disadvantages mean that some people would not want to visit Vancouver, I personally feel that most people would enjoy Vancouver.

PRONUNCIATION FOR SPEAKING

SKILLS

Connecting speech

When you speak, words often link together to make your speech flow smoothly. To do this, the sounds at the end of one word and at the beginning of another may change.

One way this happens is when you connect (link) vowels and consonants. When one word ends in a consonant sound and the next word begins with a vowel sound, there is a link between them. For example, *talk about* becomes /tɔːkəbaʊt/.

1.6 Listen to this example. Notice that the words *talk* and *about* are connected.

I'd like to talk‿about the city of Vancouver, in British Columbia, Canada.

4 1.7 Listen to the sentence below and mark the links between the consonants and vowels.

> First‿of all, let's look at some of the positives.

5 1.5 Listen and repeat the phrases in Exercise 3. Pay attention to the way you link the words together.

6 Work with a partner. Mark the links in the phrases. Then take turns saying the phrases with the linking sounds.

1 I'd like to give you some information about ...

2 Now let's talk about ...

3 The next topic is ...

4 Finally, let's look at ...

SPEAKING TASK

Give a presentation about an interesting place. Present factual information and give your opinion about the place you choose.

PREPARE

1 Look at the outline you created in Exercise 6 in the Critical thinking section. Review your notes and add any new information which you think is relevant.

2 Write a script for your introduction and conclusion. Be sure to use organizing phrases from Preparation for speaking so your audience can easily understand your presentation.

3 For each idea in your presentation, think of how you can signal facts and your opinions. You can use language like this:

Obviously, ...	In my opinion, ...
In fact, ...	I personally feel ...
As we know, ...	I think ...

4 Refer to the Task checklist below as you prepare your presentation.

TASK CHECKLIST	✔
Use the past simple correctly.	
Organize your presentation using appropriate organizing phrases.	
Only include information in your presentation that is relevant.	
Introduce facts and opinions, using the correct language.	
Join sounds in phrases when the words link together.	

PRESENT

5 Work in a group of three or four. Present your information to each other. While listening, take notes on questions that you have so you can ask them after the presentation is over.

6 Vote for the place that most students would like to visit.

OBJECTIVES REVIEW

1 Check your learning objectives for this unit. Write *3*, *2* or *1* for each objective.

3 = very well 2 = well 1 = not so well

I can …

watch and understand a video about the Grand Canal in Venice.	_____
predict content using visuals.	_____
distinguish fact from opinion.	_____
decide if ideas are relevant.	_____
use past simple statements and questions.	_____
signpost an opinion.	_____
organize information for a presentation.	_____
give a presentation about an interesting place.	_____

2 Use the *Unlock* Digital Workbook for more practice with this unit's learning objectives.

UNLOCK ONLINE

WORDLIST

ancient (adj) ⊙	cheap (adj) ⊙	recognize (v) ⊙
apartment (n)	crowded (adj)	rock (n) ⊙
area (n) ⊙	expensive (adj) ⊙	rural (adj) ⊙
be located (v) ⊙	field (n) ⊙	strange (adj) ⊙
bridge (n) ⊙	lake (n) ⊙	traffic (n) ⊙
capital (n) ⊙	modern (adj) ⊙	urban (adj) ⊙
cave (n)	popular (adj) ⊙	woods (n)

⊙ = high-frequency words in the Cambridge Academic Corpus

LEARNING OBJECTIVES	IN THIS UNIT YOU WILL ...
Watch and listen	watch and understand a video about a festival of ice sculptures in China.
Listening skills	take notes; listen for main ideas.
Critical thinking	create a persuasive argument.
Grammar	use present tense question forms; use the present continuous.
Speaking skills	make suggestions; agree and disagree.
Speaking task	choose an event from a festival and persuade your group to go to it.

FESTIVALS AND CELEBRATIONS

UNIT 2

UNLOCK YOUR KNOWLEDGE

Work with a partner. Look at the photo and answer the questions.

1 Which country do you think the festival is held in?
2 Are there any public festivals in your country which use colour?
3 A public festival is for everyone, but a private celebration is only for family and friends. What kinds of festivals and celebrations have you been to?

PLUS

WATCH AND LISTEN

PREPARING TO WATCH

ACTIVATING YOUR KNOWLEDGE

1 Work with a partner. Make a list for each question.

1 Which countries have a lot of ice and snow?
2 What are some sports and games people play on ice or in the snow?
3 What can people build from ice and snow?

PREDICTING CONTENT USING VISUALS

2 You are going to watch a video about a festival of ice and snow. Before you watch, look at the photos and read the glossary. Discuss the questions with your partner.

1 What country do you think this festival is in?
2 What is the man doing in the second photo? Where do you think the ice came from?
3 What do you think visitors can do at the festival?
4 What do you think the festival looks like at night?

GLOSSARY

sculpture (n) a piece of art that is made from stone, wood, metal, etc.

brick (n) a hard square or rectangular thing used for building walls, houses, etc.

frozen (adj) If something is frozen, it has become hard because its temperature is below 0 °C.

pure (adj) clean; not mixed with other things

skyscraper (n) a very tall building

WHILE WATCHING

UNDERSTANDING MAIN IDEAS

3 Watch the video. Write *T* (true) or *F* (false) next to the statements.

_____ 1 Harbin is having its first ice festival this year.
_____ 2 All of the ice bricks come from the river.
_____ 3 'Sun Island' is where people build snow sculptures.
_____ 4 Harbin is very cold in winter because of winds from Siberia.
_____ 5 The festival is exactly four weeks long.

4 Watch again. Complete the sentences.

UNDERSTANDING DETAIL

1 People call Harbin the ____________ .
2 Around ____________ people make the buildings and sculptures for the festival.
3 The ____________ ice bricks are made of very clean water.
4 During the day, there are sculpture classes and ____________ .
5 The average temperature in winter is – ____________ °C.
6 More than ____________ people will visit the ice festival this year.
7 The first day of the festival is ____________ .

5 Watch again. Then choose the correct photo for each word in bold.

WORKING OUT MEANING FROM CONTEXT

1 This stops air **bubbles** from freezing into the ice.

a 
b 
c 

2 There are ice castles, ice skyscrapers and ice **slides**, which are very popular with children.

a 
b 
c 

3 Visitors can play ice sports and games and see amazing **firework** shows.

a 
b 
c 

4 Until the spring comes and the Ice City **melts** away for another year.

a 
b 
c 

DISCUSSION

6 Work in a small group. Discuss the questions.

1 Would you like to go to Harbin's ice festival? Why / Why not?
2 Imagine you are going to Harbin's ice festival. Agree on a list of five to eight things to take with you. Compare your list with another group.

LISTENING

LISTENING 1

PREPARING TO LISTEN

UNDERSTANDING KEY VOCABULARY

1 You are going to listen to some interviews about three festivals. Read the sentences (1–6). Then choose the correct definition (a or b) for the words in bold.

1 We listened and took notes while the professor gave the **lecture**.
   a a book about an academic subject
   b a formal talk about a subject
2 There were many **activities** at the festival, such as watching shows or playing games.
   a things you do for enjoyment, especially organized events
   b a type of live performance in a public place
3 We wear **traditional** clothes at the festival. The clothes are very similar to the clothes my grandparents wore to the festival when they were young.
   a part of older ways of doing things and older ideas
   b relating to the present time and not to the past
4 If a festival is about **culture**, tourists often enjoy going to it because they can learn about the way of life of the local community.
   a habits and traditions of a country or group of people
   b events and activities for tourists to participate in
5 A popular type of **entertainment** at a festival is watching a race or competition.
   a shows, films, games or other ways of having fun
   b classes, lectures or other ways of learning
6 We **enjoyed** the delicious food.
   a got pleasure from something
   b did something with someone

2 Match the words in bold from Exercise 1 to the photos (a–c). In some items, more than one answer is possible.

a

b

c

________________ ________________ ________________

3 Match the festivals (1–3) to the photos (a–c) in Exercise 2.

1 The Festival of Ideas _____
2 The Muscat Festival _____
3 Cherry Blossom Festival _____

4 Work with a partner. Use the photos and the names of the festivals to predict what types of things you can do at each festival.

WHILE LISTENING

SKILLS

Taking notes

The main reason to take notes is so you can use them in the future. Taking notes helps you organize and remember information. Focus on the main points and important details. Remember that notes should be short. If you write too much, you sometimes miss the next part of the listening. Only write the most important words.

Place: ~~the festival is in~~ Muscat

5 Before you listen, practise keeping your notes short. Cross out the words that are not needed in the notes.

1 Date: The festival is in April and May.
2 Activities: You can see art and you can try cooking.

6 Compare your answers with a partner. Make changes if necessary.

TAKING NOTES ON DETAIL

7 2.1 Listen to the interviews and complete the tourist information in the festival brochure.

THE FESTIVAL OF IDEAS

Place: Cambridge, (1)__________
Month: (2)__________
Activities: learn some (3)__________ :
English Civil War (1642–1651)
learn about science: play games to find out about (4)__________ ; listen to a (5)__________ on the global economy

CHERRY BLOSSOM FESTIVAL

Place: Tokyo, Japan
Month: (6)__________
Activities: have a picnic under the cherry trees; eat at food (7)__________ ; go on the (8)__________ ; in a boat and visit (9)__________

THE MUSCAT FESTIVAL

Place: Muscat, Oman
Months: (10)__________ and (11)__________
Activities: (12)__________ : cycling, camel racing, learn traditional (13)__________ ;
go to a (14)__________ show;
eat traditional food

8 2.1 Listen again. Write *T* (true) or *F* (false) next to the statements below. Then correct the false statements.

_____ 1 The Festival of Ideas is only for students.
____

_____ 2 Both kids and adults enjoy going to the Festival of Ideas.
____

_____ 3 There aren't exact dates for the Cherry Blossom Festival.
____

_____ 4 At the Cherry Blossom Festival, people only look at the flowers.
____

_____ 5 People can learn about Oman's culture at the Muscat Festival.
____

_____ 6 Nasrra was able to go to a fashion show at the Muscat Festival.
____

DISCUSSION

9 Work with a partner. Which festivals from Exercise 7 would you like to go to? Which activities would you most like to do?

10 Are there any festivals that you would not like to go to? Why not?

PRONUNCIATION FOR LISTENING

SKILLS

Sentence stress

In English, speakers stress some of the words or syllables in a sentence. Normally, speakers stress the important words in a sentence. It is not usual to stress short words, or words which are not important.

I want to go to the fashion show.

In the example above, the important words are *go*, *fashion* and *show*, so the speaker stresses these.

11 Look at the sentence from Listening 1. Which words are important for understanding the sentence? Underline them.

Well, it's an interesting event to come to.

12 2.2 Listen to the sentence from Exercise 11. Which words are stressed?

13 Look at the questions from Listening 1. Underline the stressed words.

1 So, what kinds of things do people learn?
2 Are there any things you don't like about it?
3 Do you have many people here from other countries?

14 2.3 Listen and check. Repeat the questions.

15 Read the questions. Underline the important words.

1 What activities do people do at festivals in their free time?
2 Which festival is good for people with lots of hobbies?
3 What did you do at the Cherry Blossom Festival last weekend?

16 Work with a partner. Ask and answer the questions in Exercise 15 using the correct stress.

PLUS

LANGUAGE DEVELOPMENT

REVIEW OF PRESENT TENSE QUESTION FORMS

GRAMMAR

Yes / No questions with *do / does*

Do / Does + subject + infinitive

Do I / you / we / they like festivals? **Does he / she / it like** festivals?

Short answers:

Positive:

Yes, **I / you / we / they do**. Yes, **he / she / it does**.

Negative:

No, **I / you / we / they do not (don't)**. No, **he / she / it does not (doesn't)**.

Yes / No questions with *be*

Am / Is / Are + subject

Am I in the right place? **Is he / she / it** bored?

Are you / we / they alright?

Short answers:

Positive:

Yes, **I am**. Yes, **he / she / it is**. Yes, **you / we / they are**.

Negative:

No, **I am (I'm) not**. No, **he / she / it is not (isn't)**.

No, **you / we / they are not (aren't)**.

Wh- questions

Wh- word + *be* + subject

Where are you from?

Wh- word + *do / does* + subject + infinitive

What do you **do**? **How does** it **work**?

1 Look at the questions from Listening 1 and underline the main verbs.

1 So, what kinds of things do people learn?
2 Do people concentrate on learning just one thing?
3 Are you ever bored?

2 A presenter on a radio programme is going to interview the organizer of a food festival. Read the interview questions and correct the errors.

1 Are you like your job?
2 Do you a chef?
3 What time is the festival start?
4 What kinds of food are you have?
5 Does it all good?
6 Where are people eat their lunch?
7 Is you like the food?
8 Do the work interesting?

3 2.4 Listen and check your answers to Exercise 2.

4 Use the words to make questions in the present simple.

1 you / like / festivals?

____

2 When / you / go / home?

____

3 you / be / a good cook?

____

4 When / you / feel / hungry?

____

5 What / you / do / for fun?

____

6 you / like / your school?

____

5 Work with a partner. Compare your questions and make any corrections. Ask and answer the questions.

THE PRESENT CONTINUOUS

GRAMMAR

Use the present continuous to talk about events and actions happening at, or around, the moment of speaking.

Statements

subject + *be* + verb + *-ing*

I **am texting** my friend. You / We / They **are having** a picnic.
He / She / It **is waiting** for you outside.

Yes / No questions

be + subject + verb + *-ing*

Am I **going** the right way? **Are** you / we / they **watching** the camel race?
Is he / she / it **working**?

Short answers:

Positive:

Yes, **I am**. Yes, **you / we / they are**. Yes, **he / she / it is**.

Negative:

No, **I am (I'm) not**. No, **you / we / they are not (aren't)**.
No, **he / she / it is not (isn't)**.

Wh- questions

Wh- word + *be* + subject + verb + *-ing*

Where am I **going**? **What is** she / he / it **doing**?
What are they **studying**? **How are** you **doing**?

6 Complete the sentences and questions with the correct present continuous form of the verbs in brackets.

1 I ______________________ (study) English in the library right now.
2 She ______________________ (enjoy) the Cherry Blossom Festival in Tokyo.
3 They're not here. They ______________________ (attend) a sports event in the city centre.
4 The presenter ______________________ (give) a talk about gravity in the main hall.
5 We ______________________ (have) a great time at the art festival.
6 What ______________________ your brother ______________________ (do)? He looks very silly.
7 My friends and I ______________________ (watch) our favourite film. It's so good!
8 Where are they? ______________________ they ______________________ (park) the car?

PLUS

7 Work with a partner. Look at the festivals on page 42. Choose one festival and one activity. Tell your partner what you are doing, using the present continuous. Can your partner guess which festival you are attending?

Student A: I'm eating traditional food.
Student B: Are you visiting The Muscat Festival?
Student A: Yes, I am.

COLLOCATIONS WITH *GO TO*, *TAKE* AND *HAVE*

LANGUAGE

A collocation is a combination of two or more words that are often used together.

go to university, go to a talk, go to class

8 Label each circle with the correct words from the box to make verb + noun collocations. Some words can be used more than once.

a celebration (x2)   care (of)   university   ~~a concert~~
an event (x2)   ~~a festival~~   fun   ~~a nice time~~   a lecture (x2)
a party (x2)   part   place   ~~a photo~~   a problem   your time

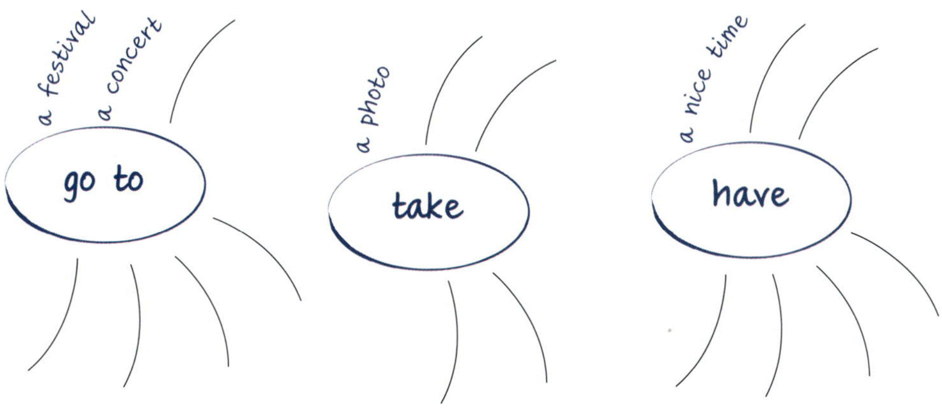

9 Complete the sentences with *go to*, *have* or *take*.

1 Excuse me, can you __________ a photo of my sister and me?
2 What time will you leave your house to __________ the celebration?
3 I'm going on holiday next week. Will you __________ care of my plants?
4 __________ a nice time on your holiday!
5 I'm sorry that I can't go to the party tonight. But I hope you __________ fun!

PLUS

10 Complete the questions with the correct form of words from Exercise 8. In some items, more than one answer is possible.

1 What do you think makes a good festival? Should everyone go to every __________ or is it OK to miss some of them?
2 Do you take __________ to enjoy a festival when you go or do you hurry to see things?
3 In your country, do people often go to __________ to listen to music?
4 If it's a special day, do you have a __________ ?

11 Work with a partner. Ask and answer the questions in Exercise 10.

LISTENING 2

PREPARING TO LISTEN

UNDERSTANDING KEY VOCABULARY

1 You are going to listen to a conversation about a holiday. Read the sentences (1–7). Then write the correct form of the words in bold next to the definitions (a–g).

1 We are having a special meal to **celebrate** my graduation.
2 The actor is wearing a **costume** in the film.
3 A traditional US Thanksgiving **dish** is candied sweet potatoes. It is made with sweet potatoes, brown sugar and butter.
4 The baker **decorated** the cake with colourful flowers made of sugar.
5 I love colourful **fireworks**, but the loud sounds scare my children.
6 In the US many people give small **gifts** to their children on their graduation day, like money or books.
7 Every year there is a big **parade** on Thanksgiving. People march down the street with giant balloons and play music.

a ____________ (n) one type of food prepared as part of a bigger meal
b ____________ (n) small objects which explode to make a loud noise and bright colours and are often used for special events
c ____________ (n) a line of people or vehicles that moves through the streets to celebrate a special day or event
d ____________ (v) to do something fun because it is a special day or because something good has happened
e ____________ (n) something special that you give to someone else
f ____________ (n) clothes that people wear to make them look like someone or something else
g ____________ (v) to make something look pretty by putting things on it

PLUS

2 Match the words in bold from Exercise 1 to the photos below. In some items, more than one answer is possible.

a

____

b

____

c

____

PREDICTING CONTENT USING VISUALS

3 Work with a partner. Which types of celebrations or holidays are related to these photos?

WHILE LISTENING

SKILLS

Listening for main ideas

Main ideas are the most important ideas about the topic being discussed. To help you understand what the main idea is, think about the topic. What aspect of the topic does the speaker focus on? For example, a main idea about the topic of festivals could be that they have a lot of fun activities. So that is what the speaker or speakers talk about. Take notes on the main ideas as you listen.

TAKING NOTES ON MAIN IDEAS

4 2.5 Listen to the conversation and write the main ideas. Remember that main ideas are the most important ideas about a topic.

North American holiday: (1)__________

US & Canada celebrate – everyone thankful

(2)__________ and friends – eat meal together

(3)__________ meal: turkey, stuffing, potatoes, corn, cranberries, pie

(4)__________ differences:

(5)__________	(6)__________
(7)__________ : spicy	sweet, whipped cream
(8)__________ : rice or bread	cornbread, oysters

(9)__________ : leaves, autumn vegetables, candles

(10)__________ (red, yellow, orange)

(11)__________ : parades, watch sports on TV; no gifts

Canadian Thanksgiving: October; American Thanksgiving: November

(12)__________ : small local parade; (13)__________ : big New York City parade on TV

Different (14)__________ for the holiday

Canada: autumn harvest

US: autumn harvest + remembering Native Americans helping settlers hunt and grow food

LISTENING FOR DETAIL

5 2.5 Listen again. Write *T* (true) or *F* (false) next to the statements below. Then correct the false statements.

_____ 1 Paul likes Thanksgiving because there are fireworks.
____

_____ 2 Potatoes, corn and cranberries are from Europe.
____

_____ 3 In the southern US, sometimes oysters are used for stuffing.
____

_____ 4 In Canada, they celebrate Thanksgiving on a Monday.
____

_____ 5 In the US, they celebrate Thanksgiving on a Thursday.
____

POST-LISTENING

RECOGNIZING EXAMPLES

6 2.6 Listen to the examples related to Thanksgiving. Complete the sentences with phrases for introducing examples.

1 ... some people prefer different kinds of pie, __________ apple.
2 ... people often decorate their dinner tables and homes with things __________ colourful leaves, autumn vegetables and candles.
3 __________ , both countries celebrate with parades with marching bands and people in costumes.
4 Well, __________ , in Canada, the holiday is celebrated on the second Monday in October.

7 Look at each phrase in Exercise 6 and answer the questions.

1 Which two ways of introducing examples can only be followed by a noun? __________ , __________
2 Which two ways of introducing examples can be followed by a subject and a verb or by a noun or phrase? __________ , __________

DISCUSSION

SYNTHESIZING

8 Work with a partner. Use ideas from Listening 1 and Listening 2 to complete the following task. Choose two of the festivals and celebrations. Think of two positives and two negatives for each one. Compare your ideas with your partner. Decide which one you would prefer to go to? Why?

SPEAKING

CRITICAL THINKING

At the end of this unit, you are going to do the speaking task below.

Choose an event from a festival and persuade your group to go to it.

UNDERSTAND

1 Read the description of National Day in the United Arab Emirates. Decide which of the four events you would like to go to.

2 Compare your ideas with a partner. Say why you made your decision.

National Day parades

If you love parades, don't miss the National Day parades! You'll see marchers in traditional costumes and people waving flags. They celebrate people from around the world living together in peace. They show the culture and traditions of many countries. Lots of groups from the community are also in the parade. If you like boats, you can watch the boat parade on the water. The boats are colourful, with Emirati decorations. On the main day, you can watch the parade under a night sky filled with fireworks. Come and enjoy it all with your family.

Tasty food

Do you like different kinds of food? Why not try Emirati food? You can try delicious dishes from all over the UAE. Or maybe you and your family would like to try some international food? There is an all-you-can-eat Lebanese lunch that you should try. Or how about eating a traditional sweet treat called *luqaimat*? What is it like? Eat some and see!

Fireworks

Fireworks *and* shopping? Yes! Come to the National Day Super Sale for both cheap shopping (with very low prices) and fireworks – on the main day, the sky will be lit up with an incredible show of noise and colour. Everyone enjoys the shopping and the show, but be sure to come early for a good place to park – it gets very busy, with lots of people.

Shows

Don't miss the shows! There are concerts with famous people from around the world. Many of the performers are national favourites, so be sure to plan your time carefully and choose the ones you like the best.

SKILLS

Creating a persuasive argument

When you want to persuade others to agree with you, you need to think about who your audience is. Choose the information that will make others agree with you. Present your ideas from the least important to the most important point. This helps you save your strongest points until last. Think about what the other side might say about your ideas. Finish by presenting your ideas again, but in different words.

EVALUATE

3 Work with the same partner as in Exercise 2. Make notes in the table about possible positives and negatives for each of the events described in the text.

events	ideas	
	positives	negatives
parades	traditional costumes	very crowded
food		
Super Sale and fireworks		
shows		

4 Discuss with the same partner as in Exercise 3. After looking at the positives and negatives of each of the events at this festival, do you have the same opinion as in Exercise 1 or have you changed your mind?

5 Look at the poster for National Day in the United Arab Emirates. The poster tries to persuade people to come to the events. What things in the poster help you to decide if you want to go or not?

NATIONAL DAY

When and where?

Location: United Arab Emirates

Time of year: December

Plan your visit now!

History of the festival

This festival began in 1972 and offers many events, including parades, fireworks, displays and delicious traditional food.

Have fun at the fort

Al Jahili Fort in Al Ain is one of the oldest places in the UAE. Listen to poetry and drumming. Watch traditional arts and try them yourself. Enjoy the day with your children. Make art, while learning about the history of the fort. Remember to try the tasty food as well.

Come to the races

Do you like winning? Join in the races. There is something for everyone, walking and running. Or maybe you prefer to watch? You can enjoy a car race and cheer your favourite driver. And, as always, amazing fireworks will celebrate the UAE!

6 Work with a partner. Look back at the table on page 52. Then, think of the possible advantages of the events in the poster above. Could you make the poster more persuasive? What would you change?

APPLY

PREPARATION FOR SPEAKING

MAKING SUGGESTIONS

SKILLS

We make suggestions when we give advice to someone. We also make suggestions when we are deciding what to do with someone.

*Visitors **should** try to go to the cake shop.*
***Why not** try this activity?*
***How about** driving to the festival?*

1 Put the words in order to make suggestions.

1 this / could / You / online / look at / .

____

2 starting / How / cake / ? / with / about

____

3 not / Why / yourself / ? / try it

____

2 Tick (✔) the phrases which make suggestions.

1 I will try that. ☐
2 How about trying this? ☐
3 Can I try this? ☐
4 I'd suggest trying this. ☐
5 Shall we try this? ☐
6 Can we think about trying this? ☐

3 Complete the table with the words and phrases for making suggestions from Exercises 1 and 2.

infinitive without *to*	verb + *-ing*
1 *You could* ______________ .	4 ______________ ?
2 ______________ ?	5 ______________ .
3 ______________ ?	6 ______________ ?

4 Complete the dialogue with words and phrases from Exercise 3. In some items, more than one answer is possible.

Man: This festival is fantastic. What do you want to do first?
Woman: (1)__________ we go to the food tent? I'd like to get some pizza.
Man: OK. Good idea. After that (2)__________ visiting the art exhibition? I'd like to see some of the paintings.
Woman: Yeah, that sounds good. Then we (3)__________ go and do a singing workshop.
Man: Oh, I'm not sure that's a good idea. I'm a terrible singer!
Woman: OK, well (4)__________ listening to the talk on poetry instead?
Man: Yeah, I'd love to! That's a great idea!
Woman: What (5)__________ we do after that?
Man: Well, by then we will probably need to go home!
Woman: Hmm, I might want to see some other things. How about having a look in the gift shop afterwards?
Man: Sure! That sounds good.

PLUS

5 Work with a partner. Read the dialogue aloud. Did you choose the same words and phrases?

AGREEING AND DISAGREEING

SKILLS

When responding to suggestions it is important to be polite, whether you agree or disagree with the suggestion. When people reply with *yes*, it is rarely on its own. When people reply with *no*, they often add other words so that they sound more polite.

Yes: That's a great idea! No: I'm not sure that's a good idea.

6 Look at the dialogue in Exercise 4. Underline the two ways to say 'no' and the four ways to say 'yes' to the suggestions.

PLUS

SPEAKING TASK

Choose an event from a festival and persuade your group to go to it.

PREPARE

1 Look at the National Day events in the Critical thinking section and your notes in Exercise 3. Decide which of the events you would and wouldn't like to attend. Think of reasons for your opinions.

2 Work with a different partner from the one you worked with in the Critical thinking section. Choose one event to go to. You will try to persuade another pair to go to that event, too.

3 Think of some phrases you can use to make suggestions about which event to go to. You can use language like this:

How about ... *Why don't we try ...* *Shall we ...* *We could ...*

4 Complete the notes to help you prepare for your discussion.

Our event is ______________________ [type of event].
It takes place in ______________ [place] *in* ______________ [month].
At the event you can ______________________ [activities].
You can (eat / drink / see / hear) ______________________.

5 Refer to the Task checklist below as you prepare for your discussion.

TASK CHECKLIST	✔
Use present simple questions and the present continuous correctly.	
Use vocabulary and collocations from this unit.	
Make suggestions.	
Present a persuasive argument.	
Agree or disagree, using appropriate language.	
Come to a final decision as a group.	

DISCUSS

6 Work with your partner from Exercise 2. Find another pair who chose a different event. Each pair should:

- describe the event and the activities.
- make suggestions about what to do and why it would be fun.

The other pair will try to persuade you to go to their event. As you listen to the other pair, you should:

- ask questions about the event.
- use appropriate language to show that you agree or disagree.

7 As a group, choose an event that everyone would like to go to.

8 As a group, tell the class which event you chose and why.

OBJECTIVES REVIEW

1 Check your learning objectives for this unit. Write *3*, *2* or *1* for each objective.

3 = very well 2 = well 1 = not so well

I can …

watch and understand a video about Harbin's ice festival.	_____
take notes.	_____
listen for main ideas.	_____
create a persuasive argument.	_____
use present tense question forms.	_____
use the present continuous.	_____
make suggestions.	_____
agree and disagree.	_____
choose an event from a festival and persuade my group to go to it.	_____

2 Use the *Unlock* Digital Workbook for more practice with this unit's learning objectives.

UNLOCK ONLINE

WORDLIST

activity (n) ⊙	entertainment (n) ⊙	have fun (phr)
celebrate (v)	fireworks (n)	lecture (n) ⊙
costume (n)	gift (n) ⊙	parade (n)
culture (n) ⊙	have a celebration (phr)	take care (of) (phr v)
decorate (v)	have a nice time (phr)	take part (phr v)
dish (n)	have a party (phr)	take place (phr v)
enjoy (v) ⊙	have a problem (phr)	traditional (adj) ⊙

⊙ = high-frequency words in the Cambridge Academic Corpus

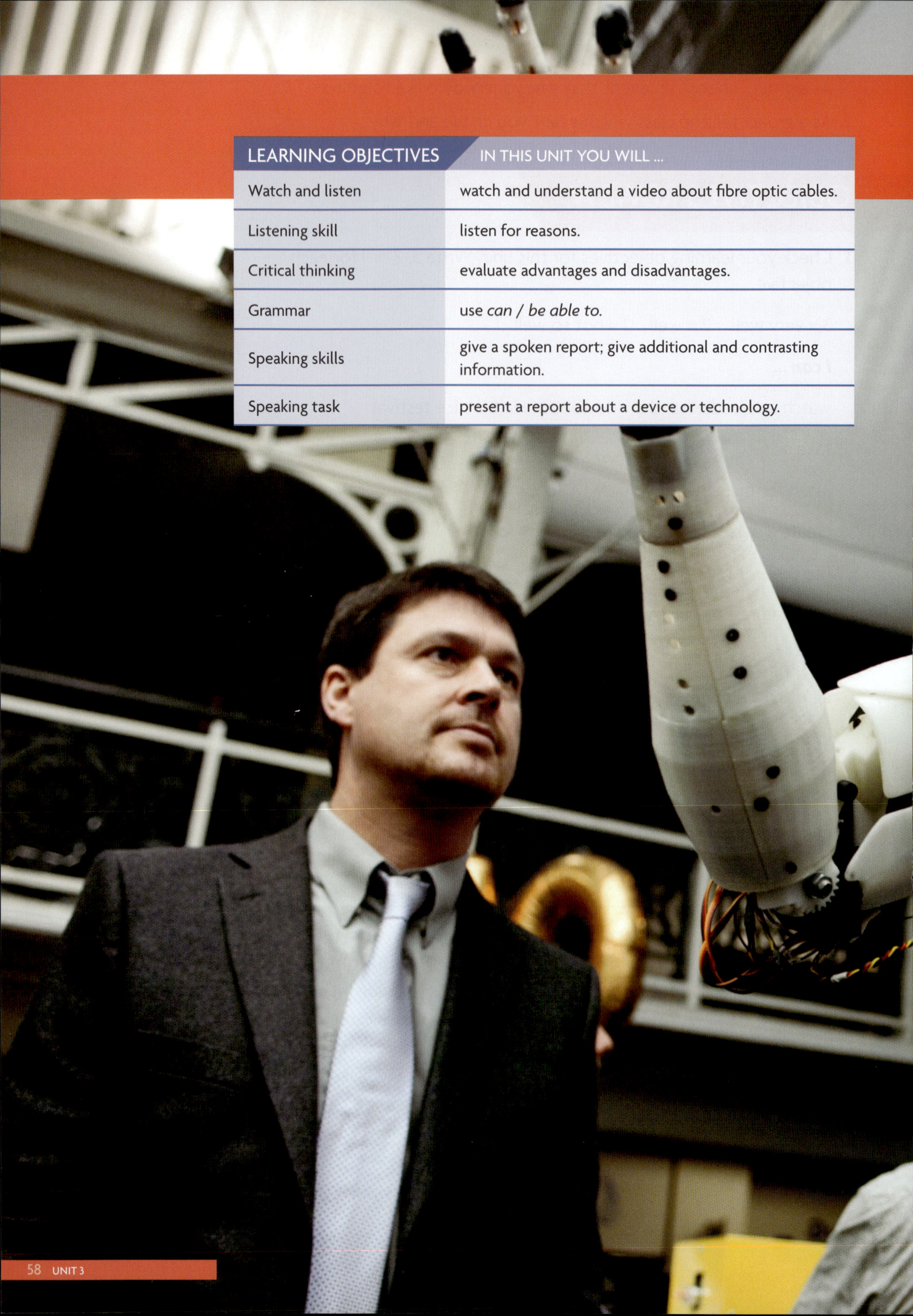

LEARNING OBJECTIVES	IN THIS UNIT YOU WILL ...
Watch and listen	watch and understand a video about fibre optic cables.
Listening skill	listen for reasons.
Critical thinking	evaluate advantages and disadvantages.
Grammar	use *can / be able to.*
Speaking skills	give a spoken report; give additional and contrasting information.
Speaking task	present a report about a device or technology.

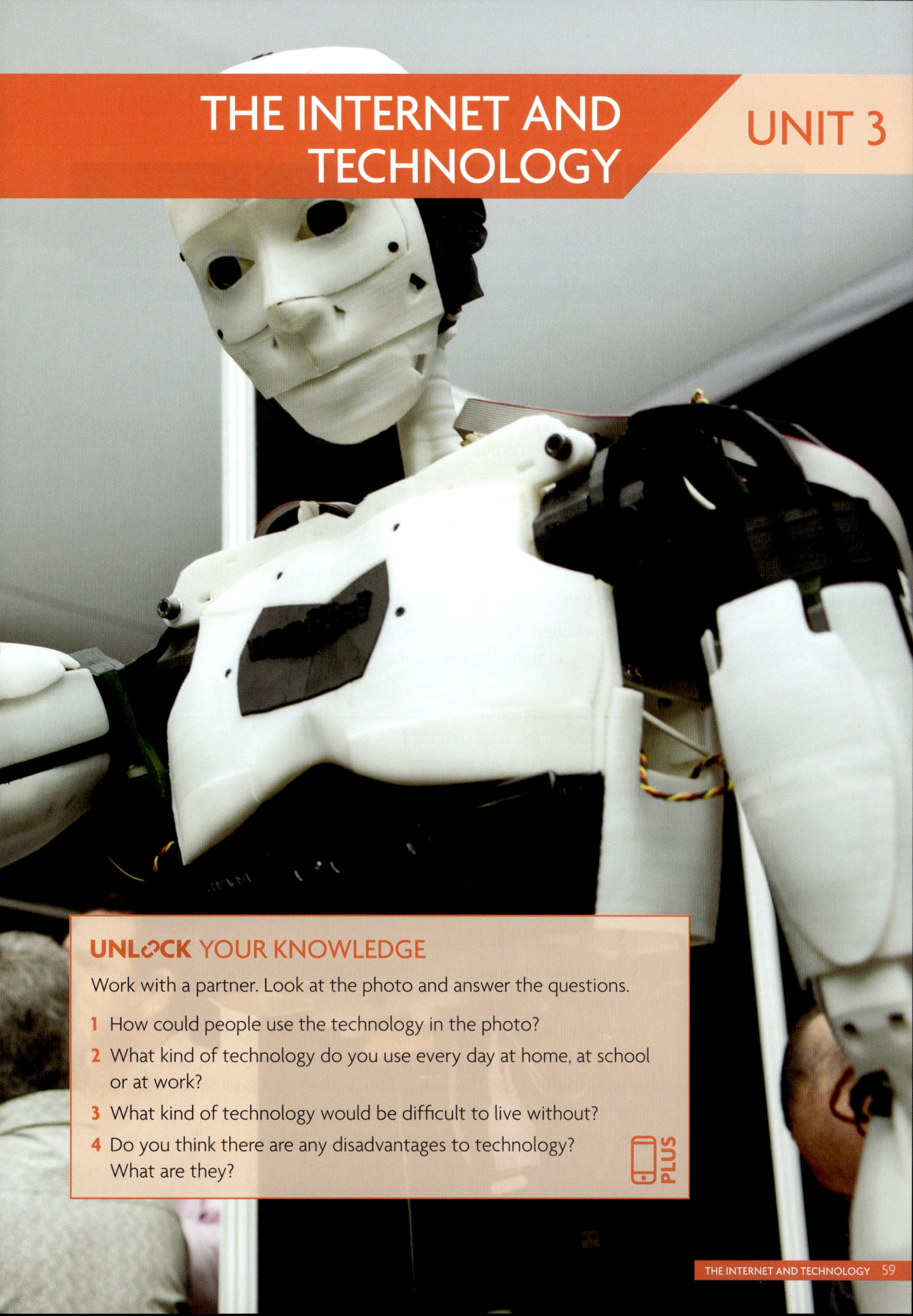

THE INTERNET AND TECHNOLOGY

UNIT 3

UNLOCK YOUR KNOWLEDGE

Work with a partner. Look at the photo and answer the questions.

1 How could people use the technology in the photo?
2 What kind of technology do you use every day at home, at school or at work?
3 What kind of technology would be difficult to live without?
4 Do you think there are any disadvantages to technology? What are they?

PLUS

WATCH AND LISTEN

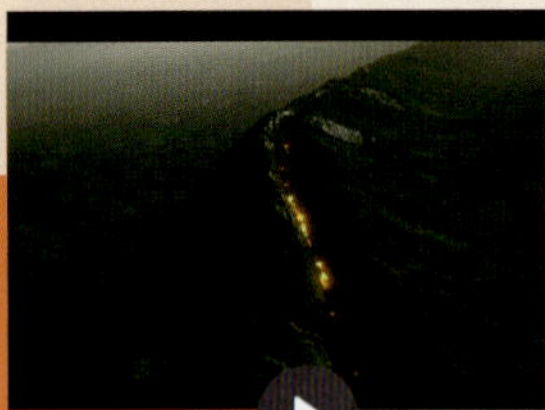
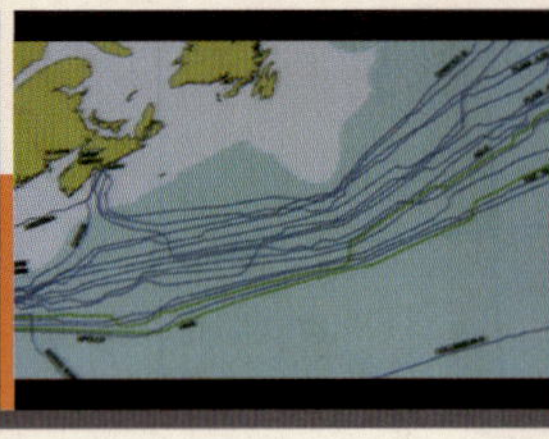

PREPARING TO WATCH

ACTIVATING YOUR KNOWLEDGE

1 Work with a partner. Answer the questions.

1 Do you mainly use the internet on a smartphone, a tablet or a computer? Why?
2 Can you remember a time when you needed the internet, but it didn't work? Why didn't it work?
3 What do people and businesses do when there is no internet?

PREDICTING CONTENT USING VISUALS

2 You are going to watch a video about the internet. Look at the photos from the video and answer the questions.

1 What problem do you think you will see in the video?
2 How do you think they will solve the problem?

GLOSSARY

violent (adj) sudden and causing damage
volcanic (adj) related to a volcano
fibre optic cables (n) very thin glass or plastic wires that carry information in phones, televisions and computer systems
go dead (phr) to stop working
crash (v) to stop working suddenly

WHILE WATCHING

UNDERSTANDING MAIN IDEAS

3 Watch the video and circle the correct answer. Compare your answers with a partner.

1 Volcanic activity *doesn't change* / *changes* the ocean floor.
2 *Most* / *Some* internet traffic goes through cables in the ocean.
3 Internet traffic goes through cables at the *top* / *bottom* of the ocean.
4 The fibre optic cables *slowly* / *suddenly* went dead.
5 *Scientists* / *Engineers* looked for the problem.
6 They found the cables were *broken* / *fixed*.
7 It took *days* / *weeks* to find and repair the cables.
8 A special kind of *ship* / *plane* helps keep the internet connected.

UNDERSTANDING DETAIL

4 Watch again. Put the sentences (a–e) in the order you hear them (1–5).

a Computers all over Asia crashed. ____
b It took weeks to find and repair the cables. ____
c Engineers looked for the problem. ____
d Important fibre optic cables ... went dead. ____
e Many people ... couldn't use the internet. ____

5 Work with a partner. Answer the questions.

1 What kind of activity happens in the middle of the ocean?
2 When did the important fibre optic cables go dead?
3 Where did the fibre optic cables go dead?
4 What moved at the bottom of the ocean and broke the cables?
5 What did they use to find and repair the cables?

MAKING INFERENCES

6 The speaker in the video asks, 'What would happen to businesses?' What do you think would happen? Circle the answer(s) that you think are possible.

a People would stop working.
b Businesses would find other ways to do business.
c Businesses would shut down.

DISCUSSION

7 Work with a partner. Discuss the questions.

1 What are some ways that people use the internet?
2 How did people do these things before the internet?
3 Do you think the internet will be different in 20 years? If so, how?

8 Work in small groups. Think about what happens when technology stops working. Complete the statements. Then compare your answers with another group.

1 When TV stops working, people can ...
2 When traffic lights stop working, drivers can ...
3 When telephones stop working, businesses can ...
4 When electric trains and metros stop working, passengers can ...

LISTENING

LISTENING 1

PREPARING TO LISTEN

UNDERSTANDING KEY VOCABULARY

1 You are going to listen to a student radio programme about robots. Read the sentences (1–8). Then choose the correct definition (a or b) for the words in bold.

1 Farah made a mistake while driving, had an **accident** and crashed her car.
   a something bad that happens, that is not on purpose and which causes injury or damage
   b something a person does on purpose which causes injury or damage to other people or things
2 The scientist **collected** water from different lakes and tested it in a lab. She found out that the water was very polluted.
   a forgot to do something at the time
   b got things from different places and brought them together
3 The company **developed** a new machine for house cleaning last year. Everyone was excited to buy it.
   a tried something new
   b made something new
4 After the car crash, Frank was **disabled** and couldn't walk anymore.
   a having an illness or injury that makes it difficult to do the things that other people can do
   b not sure of the correct way to do something
5 Some people think that taking a long holiday is a **luxury**. They don't have enough time or money to do that.
   a something expensive that you enjoy but do not need
   b something that you have never done before
6 Nowadays, **robots** are used by doctors to do surgery.
   a reports that doctors read before doing an operation
   b machines which can do things that people can do
7 People often wear a **suit** when they go for a job interview so they will look professional.
   a a particular set of clothes that has to be worn by the members of the same organization or group of people
   b an outfit of a jacket and trousers or a jacket and skirt made of the same material
8 The student needed to find **information** about how cities clean up air pollution. He looked online, found books in the library and read academic papers on the subject.
   a objects used to do scientific experiments
   b facts about a situation, person, event, etc.

2 Work with a partner. Discuss the questions.

1 What are some things that robots can do nowadays?
2 What does a robot look like?

3 What can you see in each photo?

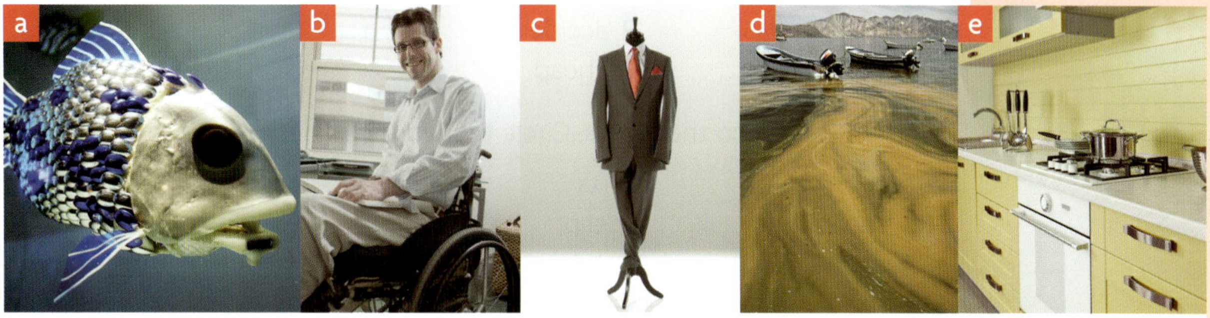

a ______________ b ______________ c ______________ d ______________ e ______________

USING YOUR KNOWLEDGE

4 Match the words from the box to the photos in Exercise 3.

disabled	fish	kitchen	pollution	suit

PRONUNCIATION FOR LISTENING

SKILLS

Consonant sounds /s/, /ʃ/, /ʧ/

The consonant sounds /s/ *subject*, /ʃ/ *show* and /ʧ/ *teacher* are easily confused. It is important to listen closely for these different sounds.

/s/ *save* /ʃ/ *shave*
/ʧ/ *watch* /ʃ/ *wash*

5 3.1 Listen to the words from Exercise 4 and the explanation box. Pay attention to the underlined sounds.

6 Work with a partner. Say the words in Exercise 4 aloud and pay attention to the underlined sounds. Then add each word to the sound maps.

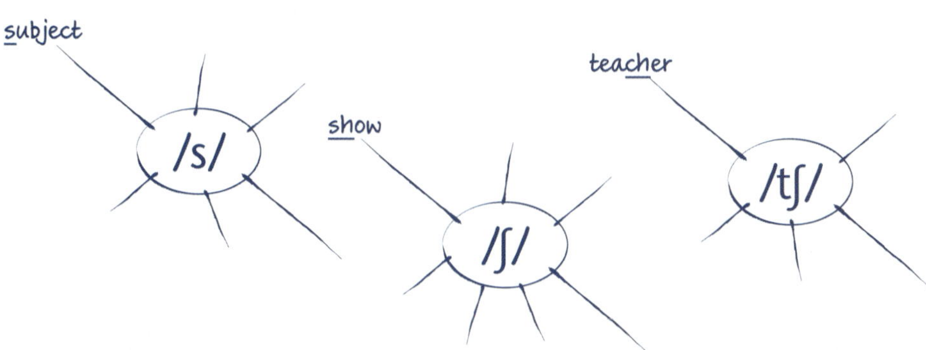

7 3.2 Listen to the words and add them to the sound maps in Exercise 6.

1 station	6 robots
2 sort	7 match
3 short	8 ocean
4 wish	9 accident
5 which	10 cheap

8 3.3 Listen to the words. Circle the word you hear.

1 shorts	sorts
2 sheep	cheap
3 wash	watch
4 sea	she
5 save	shave

9 Work with a partner. Ask and answer the questions. What else do you think robots can do?

1 What kinds of robots are there?
2 Do you think robots are cheap or expensive?
3 Can robots wash clothes?
4 Can robots measure pollution in the ocean?
5 Can robots help a disabled person shave?

TAKING NOTES ON MAIN IDEAS

WHILE LISTENING

10 3.4 Listen to the radio programme. Complete the student's notes.

Types of (1)____________ : industrial, waiter, teacher
Robots are (2)____________ now than in past, not expensive
Medical robot
Helps (3)____________ people walk after (4)____________ :
robotic (5)____________
Service robot
Saves time: does boring/dirty work, e.g. washing and cleaning
Elderly people can stay (6)____________ longer – important, not a (7)____________
Research robot
Assists scientists with (8)____________ : robotic fish
Scientists can find out about (9)____________ quickly

11 Use your notes to check your ideas in Exercise 9.

SKILLS

Listening for reasons

People often talk about reasons for things happening.

I passed my exam **because** I worked hard. (working hard is the reason I passed my exam)

When people give reasons for things, they use words and phrases like *since*, *because of*, *thanks to* and *due to*. If you hear these, you know a reason will follow.

Since there's no Wi-Fi here, I can't check my email.

I don't watch videos on my computer **because of** / **due to** the slow internet at home.

Use *thanks to* for positive reasons.

Thanks to the advice you gave me, I knew which app to use.

12 3.4 Listen to the radio programme again. Complete the reasons in the table.

event	reason
Robots weren't used very much in the past	since they were (1)________________.
Joey Abbica couldn't walk	because of an (2)________________.
People have a much better quality of life	thanks to these (3)________________.
Scientists can find out about pollution quickly	due to the (4)________________.

POST-LISTENING

13 Complete the sentences with the words in the box. In some items, more than one answer is possible.

because of	due to	since	thanks to

1 __________ Wi-Fi, Julie was able to do her work on her tablet in a café.
2 Mark couldn't use his laptop __________ a problem with the hard drive.
3 __________ he doesn't have a job, he can't buy a new laptop.
4 __________ a bad internet connection, Bill wasn't able to email me.

DISCUSSION

14 Work with a partner. Discuss the questions.

1 In what ways have robots changed society?
2 Do you think that robots are generally good or bad for us? Give reasons for your answer.
3 What kind of robot would improve your life?

PLUS

LANGUAGE DEVELOPMENT

CAN / BE ABLE TO

GRAMMAR

Statements

Use *can* (+) / *can't* (–) and *be able to* (+) / *not be able to* (–) to talk about **general ability** in the present.

Robots **can** / **are able to** help people in their everyday lives.
She **can't** / **isn't able to** do housework easily.

Use *could* (+) / *couldn't* (–) and *was able to* (+) / *wasn't able to* (–) to talk about **general ability** in the past.

Before the accident, Joey **could** / **was able to** surf really well.
After the accident, he **couldn't** / **wasn't able to** walk at all.

Use *was able to* (+) / *wasn't able to* (–) and *couldn't* (–) to talk about **ability in particular or specific situations** in the past.

He **wasn't** even **able to** sit up on his own when a visitor came.
He **was able to** stand up when he finally put on the robotic suit.
He **couldn't** feel his legs when doctors touched them.

Questions

Present: **Can you** / **Are you able to** swim?
Past: **Could you** / **Were you able to** speak both your parents' languages when you were a child?

1 Choose the correct word or phrase to complete the sentences.

1 I *am able* / *can* to swim quite well, but I don't like going under the water.
2 Mohammed *can* / *was able to* speak English and Arabic when he was a child.
3 Sunita *could* / *wasn't able to* speak for a few days after an operation in her mouth.
4 My little sister *couldn't* / *can't* hear very well when she was young.
5 Jade *wasn't able to* / *can't* open the car door, so she climbed out of the window.
6 *You are able to* / *Are you able to* speak any other languages?
7 *Can you* / *Were you able to* use a computer when you were three years old?

PLUS

2 In each box, write one ability you have now or which you had in the past.

1 speak Chinese	2 play the guitar	3
4	5	6
7	8	9

3 Work with a partner. Take turns asking about each other's ability to do the activities you wrote in Exercise 2. Use *can*, *could* or *be able to*.

Student A: Can you Speak Chinese?
Student B: Yes, I can.
Student A: Were you able play the guitar when you were young?
Student B: No, I wasn't. I started learning last year.

VOCABULARY FOR TECHNOLOGY

laptop / PC (computer)

verbs
go online log in
shut down
turn off / on

nouns
keyboard mouse
the cloud Wi-Fi

4 Complete the sentences with technology words from the word map. Use a dictionary to help you. In some items, more than one answer is possible.

1 My laptop is getting old; when I __________ it __________ , it takes a long time to start.
2 I like my touchscreen computer. Now I don't need to use the __________ to move the cursor around.
3 I can't __________ to my email because I forgot my password.
4 Do you have __________ ? I'd like to __________ and check Facebook™.
5 I've finished my essay. I could send it by email or upload it to __________ so you can download it to your computer.
6 Don't forget to __________ the laptop when you're finished.

5 Work with a partner. Discuss the questions.

1 Why is it important to have a good password? Should people use more than one password for different sites?
2 Where do you prefer to save most of your files and other important electronic information? Why?
3 How often do you use Wi-Fi?
4 What do you usually spend your time doing online?

6 Complete the word map with the words in the box. One of the words is both a verb and a noun.

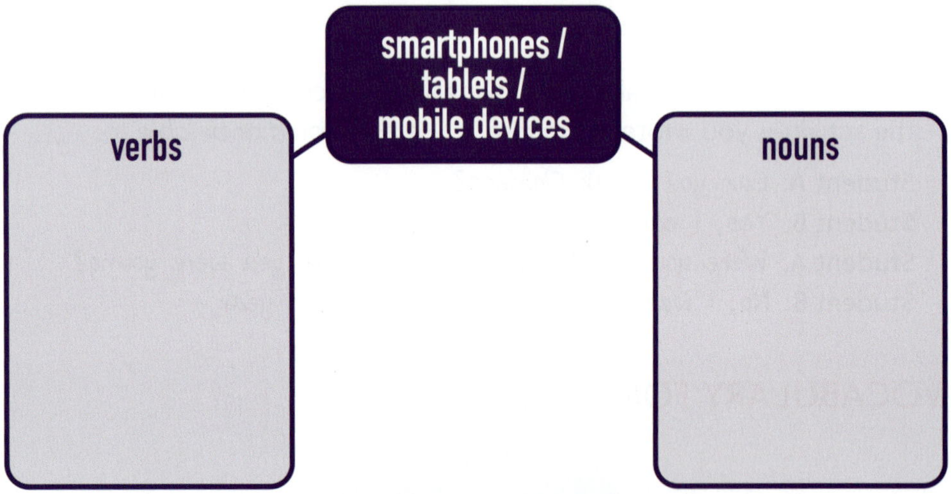

apps	battery	charge	charger	keys	surf	text

7 Complete the sentences with words from Exercise 6.

1 Do you prefer using a touchscreen or typing on real __________ . Why?
2 If you have a tablet or smartphone, which are your favourite __________ and websites? Why?
3 How often do you __________ the internet to find information? What kinds of things do you look for?
4 Do you prefer to call and talk to people or __________ them? Why?
5 Has your phone's __________ ever run out of power and stopped working at a bad time? What happened?
6 Do you take your __________ with you so you can __________ your phone at any time?

8 Work with a partner. Ask and answer the questions in Exercise 7.

PLUS

LISTENING 2

PREPARING TO LISTEN

USING YOUR KNOWLEDGE

1 Work with a partner. Discuss the questions.

1 When someone asks you a question, what is the first thing you usually do – try to think of the answer yourself or use your phone to find the answer? Why?
2 When you need to find something out, do you prefer to use your phone or ask a friend? Why?
3 How could using a computer to help you find information change the way your brain works?

UNDERSTANDING KEY VOCABULARY

2 You are going to listen to a news report about how computers affect our memory. Read the sentences (1–5). Then write the words in bold next to the definitions (a–e).

1 Sometimes I feel **stupid** when I can't remember something easily.
2 It is important to have a good **memory** when you are learning a new language. That way you don't forget the new words that you learn.
3 The scientists at my university do important **research** into tropical diseases.
4 Sometimes it's hard to remember where you put your things. It's easy to forget the **location**.
5 The **file** was damaged and I couldn't open my essay anymore. I should have made a copy.

a __________ (n) a detailed study of a subject to learn more about it
b __________ (adj) silly or not intelligent
c __________ (n) a collection of information stored in one place on a computer
d __________ (n) a place where something is found
e __________ (n) the ability to remember

PLUS

PRONUNCIATION FOR LISTENING

SKILLS

Strong /æ/ and weak /ə/

Strong /æ/ and weak /ə/ are easily confused sounds. The letter *a* is often pronounced as the strong sound /æ/ when it is stressed.

That's /ðæts/ the new app /æp/ I bought.

The letter *a* can also be pronounced /ə/ when it is not stressed. Short words like prepositions and conjunctions often contain the weak sound /ə/.

I have a /ə/ laptop and /ənd/ a /ə/ tablet.

3 3.5 The reporter in the news report you are going to listen to uses linking words to add supporting examples or details to the key information. Listen to the sentences and underline the linking words.

1 You will hear the main ideas and some additional information.
2 You will hear the main ideas as well as some additional information.

4 Work with a partner. Say the sentences in Exercise 3 aloud and pronounce the sounds correctly.

5 Work with a partner. Answer the questions. Think about the sounds in the linking words.

1 Which letter do we often not pronounce when we say *and*?
2 Is the letter *a* in *and* strong /æ/ or weak /ə/?
3 Is the letter *a* in the phrase *as well as* strong /æ/ or weak /ə/?

WHILE LISTENING

TAKING NOTES ON MAIN IDEAS

6 3.6 Listen to the report. Complete the 'main ideas' column of the notes.

main ideas	additional details
Scientists looked, in particular, at how computers affect our (1)__________ .	They wanted to find out if computers have changed the way we remember (6)__________ and knowledge.
What we think when we are asked (2)__________ questions has changed due to (3)__________ like Google™.	In the past, people tried to think of the (7)__________ to the question. Now people think about (8)__________ to find the answer. e.g. They think about what they might (9)__________ into Google™.
The type of (4)__________ we remember has changed.	People now forget (10)__________ , especially if they know the information will be saved on a computer. They remember the (11)__________ of the fact.
Computers are not making us stupid, but they are making us (5)__________ .	We are spending time remembering where to (12)__________ information but not on remembering the information itself.

LISTENING FOR DETAIL

7 3.6 Listen again. Complete the 'additional details' column of the notes.

DISCUSSION

8 Write down one type of information you keep:

a on your computer __________ .
b on your smartphone __________ .
c in the cloud __________ .

9 Compare your answers to Exercise 8 with a partner.

I keep my photos in the 'Images' file on my phone and my essays in the 'College' file on my laptop.

SYNTHESIZING

10 Work with a partner. Use ideas from Listening 1 and Listening 2 to answer the following questions.

1 What can happen to information on your computer or in the cloud?
2 Do you think that robots will make people lazy? Why / Why not?
3 What are some ways people could change how they do things if robots become part of daily life?

SPEAKING

CRITICAL THINKING

At the end of this unit, you are going to do the speaking task below.

Present a report about a device or technology. Look at advantages and disadvantages and give details to support the main ideas.

SKILLS

Evaluating advantages and disadvantages

Evaluating advantages and disadvantages is a useful academic skill. When you compare advantages and disadvantages, use your own ideas. How important is each advantage and disadvantage? Just because there are more advantages, for example, does not mean they are better than the disadvantages.

EVALUATE

1 Look at the opinions about using computers. Decide if they are advantages (+) or disadvantages (–) and add them to the correct column in the table.

1 People forget facts that are stored on computers.
2 People remember where and how to find facts.
3 Computers aren't making us stupid.
4 Computers are making us lazy.
5 People aren't trying to remember information anymore.

main argument: *Computers have changed the way we remember information.*	
advantages (+)	disadvantages (–)

2 Compare your ideas with a partner. Add more advantages and disadvantages to the table.

ANALYZE

3 Work with a partner. Choose one of the kinds of technology from the box and write it in the main argument at the top of the table. Then add some advantages and disadvantages to the table.

internet TV	smartphones	tablets	the cloud	the internet	video conferencing

main argument:

Technology, such as ____________________, can affect our day-to-day lives.

advantages (+)	disadvantages (–)

EVALUATE

4 Work with a partner who chose the same kind of technology. Do you have the same or different ideas? Add good ideas to your table.

5 Look at the table above again. Are the advantages of your technology more important than the disadvantages, or the other way around?

PREPARATION FOR SPEAKING

GIVING ADDITIONAL AND CONTRASTING INFORMATION

LANGUAGE

When you link phrases and sentences that give additional information, use linking words and phrases of addition, such as *and*, *also*, *as well as* and *too*.

I use my smartphone to talk to my friends **and** to read the news.

When you link phrases and sentences that have different or contrasting ideas, use linking words and phrases of contrast, such as *however*, *but* and *on the other hand*.

I use a smartphone, **but** my mother doesn't.

Note: When you begin a sentence with *However* or *On the other hand*, put a comma after it in writing.

I use a smartphone. **However,** my mother doesn't.
The company's new tablet has a great design. **On the other hand,** it is difficult to use.

1 Complete the sentences with the words from the box. In some items, more than one answer is possible.

but	however	on the other hand

1 When people were asked difficult questions in the past, scientists believe they tried to think of the answer to the question. ______________________, because of modern technology, the first thing people think about now is how to find the answer ...

2 For example, they think about what they might put into Google™, ______________________ in the past they thought about the question itself.

3 ... it seems that people now forget facts, especially if they know the information will be saved in a file. ______________________, an advantage is they remember the location of the fact: in other words, where to find it.

4 In conclusion, it seems that computers are not making us stupid, ______________________ they are making us lazy!

2 3.7 Listen and check your answers to Exercise 1. Remember, some sentences have more than one possible answer. Make a note of what you hear.

3 Circle the correct option to complete the rule about the words in bold.

But, **however** and **on the other hand** link *similar ideas* / *different information*.

4 Read the sentences. Do the words in bold introduce different information or additional information? __________

a People use computers to save information **and** to organize it.
b People use computers to save information **and also** to organize it.
c **Also**, people use computers to save information and to organize it.
d People use computers to save information **as well as** to organize it.
e People use computers to save information and to organize it, **too**.

5 Choose the correct linking words and phrases to complete the two sentence endings.

1 Computers help people look for things *and* / *, but*
__________ a they can find information quickly.
__________ b they can make people lazy.
2 Technology is now important for our social lives *and also* / *, but*
__________ a traditional activities like writing letters are disappearing.
__________ b makes it easier for us to communicate with friends.
3 Robots assist people with difficult jobs *as well as* / *. However,*
__________ a helping take care of elderly and disabled people.
__________ b some people believe they are bad because people lose their jobs when robots are used.

PLUS

GIVING A SPOKEN REPORT

SKILLS

To prepare a spoken report, gather information and make sure it is true. Choose interesting or surprising facts. Choose only two or three main points to talk about. Be sure to give some details or facts for each main point. But do not use too much information or your listener might have difficulty understanding it.

Organize your presentation. Have a short, interesting introduction. What does your audience already know? What information do you need to explain before you start? Explain why you are giving your report. Finish by stating your main point again, using different words.

6 Read the explanation box above. Which introduction (1) and conclusion (2) is better, *a* or *b*?

1 a Today I am going to present my report on mobile phones. A mobile phone is a device for texts, calls and many other things. The main argument I am going to present is that many people have phones today.
b Today I am going to present my report on mobile phones. Mobile phones are very useful, but not everyone should have one. The main argument I am going to present is that children under the age of 14 should not own mobile phones.

2 a In conclusion, that is all I have to say. I hope you enjoyed my presentation about how many people have mobile phones. Thank you very much.

b To conclude, there are many reasons why children should not have mobile phones. The facts in support of this idea are very strong. I hope people will think about this.

7 Work with a partner. Discuss your reasons for your answers to Exercise 6.

8 Read sentences *a* and *b* and think about the function of the phrases in bold. Then circle the correct word to complete the sentence below.

a **To conclude**, we have seen that computers are a useful way to store information, but you have to remember where you store it and how to find it again!

b **In conclusion**, we have seen that computers are a useful way to store information, but you have to remember where you store it and how to find it again!

We use these expressions to *introduce / finish* what we are saying in a report.

PLUS

SPEAKING TASK

Present a report about a device or technology. Look at advantages and disadvantages and give details to support the main ideas.

PREPARE

1 Look at the advantages and disadvantages you wrote about technology in the Critical thinking section on page 74. Complete these sentences with your ideas to start your report.

Today I am going to present my report on ______________________
(Write the name of the technology.)
The main argument I am going to present is ______________________

____

(Write the main argument from your table.)

2 Write sentences about the main argument and give reasons to support your opinions. You can use language like this:

because of   due to   since   thanks to

3 Give additional and contrasting information. Connect this information using linking words and phrases like this:

also   and   and also   as well as   too   but   however
on the other hand

Computers are important because they have changed the way we remember information. People aren't trying to remember information anymore. **Also**, they forget facts that are stored on computers, **but** they remember where and how to find facts. Computers aren't making us stupid. **However**, computers are making us lazy.

4 Add a sentence to finish your presentation. You can use language like this:

In conclusion ...   To conclude ...

5 Refer to the Task checklist below as you prepare your presentation.

TASK CHECKLIST	✔
Use *can* and *be able to* correctly.	
Use words and phrases for giving reasons.	
Offer main ideas and supporting details using the correct language.	
Present advantages and disadvantages.	
Link sentences using linking words and phrases to contrast ideas or add extra information.	

PRACTISE

6 Practise the introduction to your report, the sentences about advantages and disadvantages and the conclusion.

PRESENT

7 Present your report to a partner and listen to their presentation. Discuss each of your ideas. Do you agree or disagree with your partner's ideas about their technology? Why / Why not?

OBJECTIVES REVIEW

1 Check your learning objectives for this unit. Write *3*, *2* or *1* for each objective.

3 = very well 2 = well 1 = not so well

I can ...

watch and understand a video about fibre optic cables.	_____
listen for reasons.	_____
evaluate advantages and disadvantages.	_____
use *can / be able to*.	_____
give a spoken report.	_____
give additional and contrasting information.	_____
present a report about a device or technology.	_____

2 Use the *Unlock* Digital Workbook for more practice with this unit's learning objectives.

UNLOCK ONLINE

WORDLIST

accident (n) ⊙
app (n)
battery (n)
charge (v) ⊙
charger (n)
collect (v) ⊙
develop (v) ⊙
disabled (adj) ⊙
file (n) ⊙
go online (phr)
information (n) ⊙
key (n) ⊙
keyboard (n)
laptop (n)
location (n) ⊙
log in (v)
luxury (n)
memory (n) ⊙
mouse (n) ⊙
PC (n) ⊙
research (n) ⊙
robot (n) ⊙
shut down (v)
stupid (adj)
suit (n) ⊙
surf the internet (phr)
text (n, v) ⊙
the cloud (n)
turn off (v)
turn on (v)
Wi-Fi (n)

⊙ = high-frequency words in the Cambridge Academic Corpus

LEARNING OBJECTIVES	IN THIS UNIT YOU WILL ...
Watch and listen	watch and understand a video about the impact of oceans on climate.
Listening skill	predict ideas from research.
Critical thinking	evaluate effects.
Grammar	use gerunds and infinitives; use future forms.
Speaking skill	use linking words to explain cause and effect.
Speaking task	give a presentation about climate change.

WEATHER AND CLIMATE

UNIT 4

UNLOCK YOUR KNOWLEDGE

Work with a partner. Look at the photo and answer the questions.

1 Do you get weather like this in your country? What kind of weather do you get?

2 How has the weather in your country changed? How does it affect people?

3 Have you ever experienced very bad or dangerous weather conditions? What were they? What did you do differently because of this weather?

PLUS

WATCH AND LISTEN

PREPARING TO WATCH

ACTIVATING YOUR KNOWLEDGE

1 Work with a partner. Answer the questions.

1 How many oceans are there in the world? Can you name them?
2 How much of the Earth is covered by water?
3 Do you think oceans are important? Why / Why not?

PREDICTING CONTENT USING VISUALS

2 Look at the diagram of Earth. Write a, b, c, d or e in the statements below. Then compare your answers with a partner.

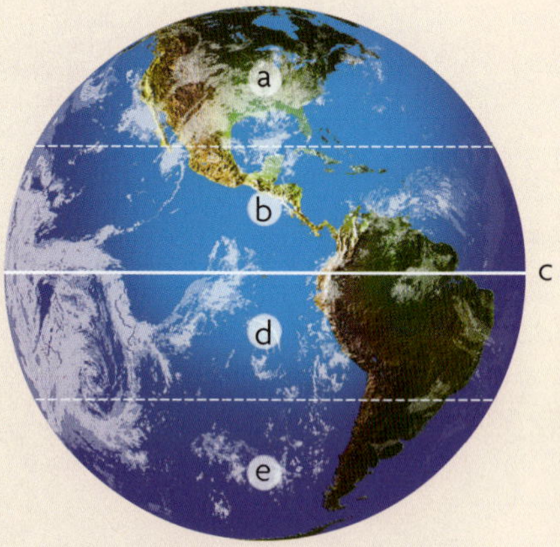

1 The weather is usually warm and sunny in _____ , _____ and _____ .
2 The weather in _____ and _____ is usually cold in winter.
3 Places near _____ are the hottest.
4 My country's weather is similar to the weather in _____ .

GLOSSARY

current (n) a movement of water or air

gyre (n) a flow of water in a circle

the equator (n) the imaginary line around the Earth that divides it into equal north and south parts

clockwise (adv) in the same direction as the hands on a clock move

heat (n) hot weather; extreme warmth

WHILE WATCHING

UNDERSTANDING DETAIL

3 Watch the video. Which parts of the diagram in Exercise 2 show:

1 the equator?
2 the area north of the equator?
3 the area south of the equator?
4 the west coast of Chile in South America?

4 Write *T* (true) or *F* (false) next to the statements below. Then watch the video again and check your answers.

_____ 1 Water covers almost 50% of the Earth.
_____ 2 The water in the oceans moves around the planet.
_____ 3 Ocean gyres are small circles of currents in the ocean.
_____ 4 South of the equator, currents move clockwise.
_____ 5 These ocean currents keep water and heat in the same place.
_____ 6 Energy and heat from the equator changes our climate.
_____ 7 10% of the fish we eat comes from a small part of the ocean near Chile.

UNDERSTANDING MAIN IDEAS

5 Match the sentence halves. Then compare your answers with a partner. Watch the video again and check your answers.

1 Water in the oceans moves because _____
2 Ocean gyres are important to the climate because _____
3 There is warmer weather north of the equator because _____
4 South of the equator, ocean gyres are important because _____
5 It's a perfect place for fish to live because _____

a this water has lots of food in it.
b the Earth is spinning.
c warmer water from the equator moves north.
d they move water and heat.
e they move cooler water north along Chile in South America.

MAKING INFERENCES

6 Work with a partner. The speaker in the video says that 'without these ocean gyres, our world would be a very different place'. What does the speaker mean?

DISCUSSION

7 Work with a partner or in small groups. Discuss the effects that heat has on:

a the clothes we wear.
b the food we eat.
c the homes we live in.

LISTENING

LISTENING 1

PRONUNCIATION FOR LISTENING

SKILLS

Rising and falling intonation to understand mood

Intonation describes how the tone of your voice goes up (rises) and goes down (falls). Intonation can help you understand someone's mood (happy, interested, excited, bored, sad, upset, etc.). Rising intonation can show interest, happiness or enthusiasm. Falling intonation often shows boredom, sadness or lack of enthusiam.

really = The speaker is interested.

really = The speaker is bored or not interested.

The meaning of a sentence can change depending on the intonation. Read the sentence aloud with a rising intonation and then a falling intonation. How does the meaning change?

I know.

1 4.1 Listen to the dialogues. Write *I* (interested) or *N* (not interested) for Speaker B.

1 A: Did you know global warming is still increasing?
  B: Is it? ______
2 A: It's my birthday today.
  B: Really? Happy birthday! ______
3 A: The weather got really chilly, didn't it?
  B: I suppose so. ______
4 A: Thanks for inviting me to your party!
  B: You're welcome. It'll be nice to see you! ______
5 A: Dinner was great.
  B: Good. Glad you liked it. ______

2 Work with a partner. Read the dialogues in Exercise 1 aloud. Speaker B should change their intonation. Speaker A should guess whether Speaker B sounds interested or bored. Why is it important to notice a speaker's intonation? Why is it important to pay attention to your own intonation?

PREPARING TO LISTEN

UNDERSTANDING KEY VOCABULARY

3 Read the definitions. Then complete the sentences with the correct form of the words in bold.

> **angry** (adj) having a strong feeling that makes you want to shout at someone or hurt them
> **cool** (adj) slightly cold; of a low temperature
> **dry** (adj) without water or liquid
> **energy** (n) the power and ability to do something or be active
> **humid** (adj) having a lot of moisture in the air
> **prefer** (v) to choose or want one thing instead of another
> **upset** (adj) unhappy or worried because something unpleasant has happened

1 The weather was very hot and ________ today. People were sweating a lot because the air was very wet.
2 When it doesn't rain and the weather is very ________ , people worry that plants will die. There isn't enough water to help them grow.
3 I was ________ when it rained during my party in the park because the rain made all the food wet. No one was having fun outside.
4 I like ________ weather because it's nice and relaxing. Hot weather makes me feel ill.
5 When the sun isn't out, some people feel tired and don't have ________ to get things done.
6 Some people get ________ in very hot weather. They become unfriendly and unpleasant because the heat is too much to take.
7 Which type of weather do you ________ ? Do you like rainy weather or sunny weather?

USING YOUR KNOWLEDGE

4 You are going to listen to a discussion between two students who have been asked to prepare a survey about the weather and how it changes people's moods. Work with a partner. How do you think different types of weather affect people's moods? Do you and your partner agree? Why / Why not?

WHILE LISTENING

TAKING NOTES ON MAIN IDEAS

5 4.2 Listen to part 1 of the discussion about weather and its effects on mood. Complete Sergio's notes on the ideas map.

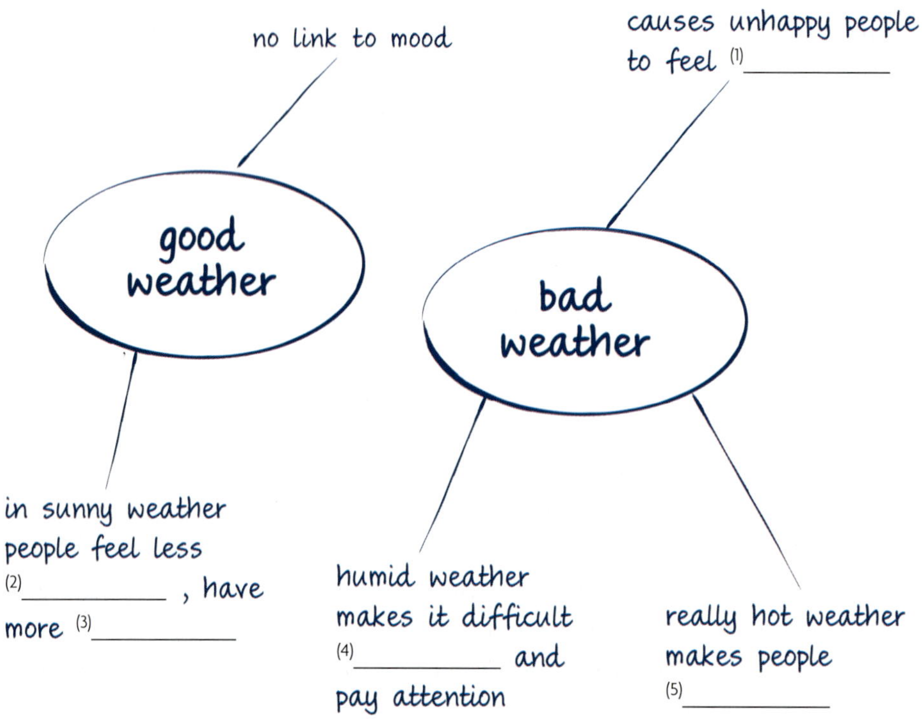

LISTENING FOR DETAIL

6 4.2 Sergio and Murat have to choose the topic that they think is the most important. Match the topics (1–4) to the reasons (a–d) for choosing or not choosing them. Then listen again and check your answers.

1 sunny weather
2 humid weather
3 bad weather
4 really hot weather

a wrong topic: not about feelings
b not sure if the facts are true
c final choice: Murat preferred it
d final choice: Murat didn't like it

7 4.3 Listen to the results of the survey in part 2. Circle the correct answer.

1 *Fourteen* / *Fifteen* people prefer sunny weather to rainy weather.
2 *Twelve* / *Thirteen* people said that they could get more done when there was sunshine.
3 Fourteen people said they have more energy when it is *light* / *dark*.
4 Sergio thinks the survey shows people have *more* / *less* energy when the weather is good.

DISCUSSION

8 Work with a partner. Discuss the questions. Ask your partner follow-up questions.

1 Can you think of an example when weather has changed your mood?
2 Would it be easy for you to live in another country if the weather there was very different from the weather in your country?

LANGUAGE DEVELOPMENT

VERB COLLOCATIONS

1 Match the verbs (1–5) to the nouns (a–e) to make collocations. In some items, more than one answer is possible. Use a dictionary to help you.

1 save	a research
2 prevent	b forest fires
3 do	c trees
4 cut down	d global warming
5 cause	e wildlife

2 Complete the sentences with the correct form of the verbs from Exercise 1.

1 We should __________ forest fires by putting out campfires.
2 We should __________ the plants in our garden if they get too big.
3 We should __________ wildlife that is in danger of disappearing.
4 Scientists need to __________ more research about the rainforests.
5 Large amounts of carbon dioxide __________ global warming.

PLUS

GERUNDS AND INFINITIVES

GRAMMAR

When two verbs come together, the second verb is usually an infinitive (*to* + verb) or a gerund (verb + *-ing*). When you learn a new verb, it is important to learn the structures that can follow it.

We **want** **to learn** more about global warming. (*to* + verb)
I **enjoy** **learning** about science. (verb + *-ing*)

verbs followed by an infinitive (*to* + verb)	verbs followed by a gerund (verb + *-ing*)	verbs followed by an infinitive or a gerund
decide	enjoy	begin
hope	finish	continue
learn	keep	hate
need	stop	like
plan		love
want		prefer
		start

3 Choose the correct form of the verbs in the sentences. Sometimes both are correct.

1 I enjoy *to learn* / *learning* about weather.
2 We need *to think* / *thinking* of a research question.
3 Some people prefer *to visit* / *visiting* places with lots of wildlife.
4 My mother and father want *to watch* / *watching* a film about rainforests.
5 I decided *to go* / *going* to the mountains.
6 After we finish *to listen* / *listening* to the presentation, we'll go home.
7 I plan *to study* / *studying* more about global warming.
8 Scientists began *to tell* / *telling* us about their research years ago.

4 Complete the sentences with the infinitive or gerund form of the verbs in brackets. In some items, more than one answer is possible.

1 I started __________ (learn) about weather patterns because I'm very interested in science.
2 She wanted __________ (go) to the Amazon rainforest.
3 I don't like __________ (read) research. I prefer __________ (attend) presentations.
4 He decided __________ (study) weather and people's moods.
5 What time will the presenter finish __________ (talk) about global warming?

6 I enjoy __________ (walk) in the mountains this time of year because the weather is really good.
7 I hope __________ (visit) Japan next year.
8 I really like __________ (watch) birds in the woods. I think they are very interesting.
9 The organizers will continue __________ (invite) important scientists to the conference every year.

5 Compare your answers to Exercise 4 with a partner.

FUTURE FORMS

GRAMMAR

Decisions and plans

Use *will* to talk about decisions made at the time you are speaking.
I didn't know how much damage plastics do to the environment. From now on, I **will** try to recycle more.

Use *be going to* + infinitive to talk about decisions made before you speak or a general plan that can change in the future.
Biju **is going to** present information about the forests next week.

Use *the present continuous* (*be* + verb + *-ing*) to talk about fixed arrangements made for the future. It is difficult to change these arrangements.
Next week, many people **are meeting** to talk about protecting the climate and saving the rainforests.

Predictions

Use *will* when you are certain about a future event. Use *probably* after *will* when you are a bit less certain.
Some scientists have claimed that next year **will** be the hottest for over a decade.
We need to plan now or we **will probably** lose some species completely.

Use *be going to* + infinitive to talk about a future event when there is evidence.
In fact, scientists believe 45 percent of forest areas **are going to** change completely in the next 80 years.

You can often use either *will* or *be going to* for predictions with a very similar meaning.
Sea levels **will** / **are going to** rise over the next 50 years.

6 Complete the sentences with the correct future form of the verbs in brackets. In some items, more than one answer is possible.

Decisions and plans

1 I've just finished packing. I ____________________ (leave) tonight at six o'clock to catch the train.

2 I haven't finished my project on global warming because I don't have enough information. I decided that I ____________________ (do) some more research online.

3 A: I ____________________ (go) to the garden centre this weekend. Does anyone want to come?
B: OK, I ____________________ (come) with you.

4 Professor Lang ____________________ (talk) about global warming in her lecture tomorrow.

Predictions

5 You are carrying too many books! You ____________________ (drop) them.

PLUS

6 I think we ____________________ (be) very sorry about how we treat the planet one day.

7 Write sentences about you for each of the statements.

1 something I am doing this weekend
I'm going walking with my friends in the mountains.

2 a prediction I think will come true in the next year
____

3 something I am going to do in my studies or at work in the future
____

4 an event I'm planning to go to this week
____

8 Work with a partner. Take turns telling each other about your plans and predictions in Exercise 7.

LISTENING 2

PRONUNCIATION FOR LISTENING

SKILLS

Vowel sounds /ɒ/ and /əʊ/

Two easily confused vowel sounds are /ɒ/ and /əʊ/. You can hear the sound /ɒ/ in words like o̲n and jo̲b. You can hear the sound /əʊ/ in words like go̲ and co̲ld.

1 Say the words in groups A and B aloud. Which sound can you hear in each group? Write *1* (ɒ) or *2* (əʊ).

A ________	frog	stop	cost	want
B ________	global	don't	known	won't

2 Work with a partner. Complete the sentences with words from Exercise 1. Not every word will be used.

1 We ________ have a rainy season in my country. It's usually very dry.
2 Most people in my country ________ to stop climate change, but they don't know how.
3 I don't know if it is possible to ________ global warming or if it's too late.
4 People have ________ about global warming for a long time, but they haven't done much about it.
5 If we want to stop global warming, it will ________ a lot of money.

3 Take turns saying the sentences in Exercise 2 aloud. Then decide if sentences 1–3 are true or false for you.

PREPARING TO LISTEN

PREDICTING CONTENT USING VISUALS

4 You are going to listen to a news report about global warming. Look at the photo of an animal mentioned in the report. Which type of animal do you think it shows? What kind of weather do you think an animal like this needs?

UNDERSTANDING KEY VOCABULARY

5 Read the information about the Western Ghats rainforest. Then write the correct form of the words in bold next to the definitions below.

The Western Ghats is a mountain range in western India, and it is home to four tropical and subtropical rainforests. The rainforests have a short dry period each year, but typically they get a lot of rain. However, the type of weather in the rainforests is changing quickly and global warming means that nowadays less rain falls. This is changing the rainforests themselves; the environment is **becoming** damaged and the plants and trees are growing more slowly. The rainforests are home to **unusual** wildlife[1], which looks nothing like any other wildlife on Earth, and scientists are still **discovering** new species[2]. However, the damage to the rainforests means that some animals which can't be found anywhere else are **disappearing** because they are being killed by the changes in the climate. Many people **believe** that governments need to **save** the rainforests so that they will still be around in the future. They say it is important to **look after** the forests and the animals so that climate change won't kill them. Researchers will have to look **carefully** for ways to stop global warming. They will need to really watch what is happening, take time to do research and think about whether the possible solutions will help or not.

[1]**wildlife** (n) animals and birds living in the natural environment
[2]**species** (n) groups of plants or animals with similar characteristics

1 ________ (v) to think that something is true and correct
2 ________ (v) to take care of someone or something by keeping them healthy or in a good condition
3 ________ (v) to stop existing in the world
4 ________ (adv) with great attention
5 ________ (v) to find something for the first time
6 ________ (v) to begin to be something
7 ________ (adj) different from what is common or expected
8 ________ (v) to bring something back to good condition; to keep something from harm

PLUS

USING YOUR KNOWLEDGE

6 Summarize the information from Exercise 5. Choose three key points.

Key points
1
2
3

7 Work with a partner. Compare your key points from Exercise 6. Did you choose the same points?

SKILLS

Predicting ideas from research

Before you listen to lectures, reports or information about a topic, you often have time to prepare. It helps to read some information in advance. This can help you learn about the key topic and issues that people think are important. You can then predict the main ideas that you will hear.

8 You are going to listen to a news report connected to global warming and the text in Exercise 5. Look at the text in Exercise 5 again and circle the points below that you think you will hear in the news report.

1 city names
2 information about the weather in the rainforest
3 facts about wildlife
4 the typical day of a scientist
5 information about the effects of global warming

9 Compare your answers with a partner. Were they the same? If not, discuss and agree on your answers.

WHILE LISTENING

TAKING NOTES ON MAIN IDEAS

10 4.4 Listen to the news report. Complete the notes on the causes and effects. Check your predictions from Exercise 8.

Cause		Effect
– Global warming	→	– Creates (1) __________ in rainforests in India
– (2) __________ down trees	→	– (3) __________ forests more
– Worse global warming – Increased temperature	→	– Stops normal forest growth, trees disappear
– Rainforests get less (4) __________	→	– Changes how forests work
– Governments are not stopping damage to forests fast enough	→	– In next 80 years (5) __________ % of forest areas will change
– If we don't stop damage to forests	→	– Purple frog will (6) __________

LISTENING FOR DETAIL

11 4.4 Listen again. Circle the correct answer.

1 Trees help prevent global warming because they ...
   a take in carbon dioxide. **b** stop rainfall.

2 Scientists believe ...
   a governments are actively damaging the rainforests. **b** governments are not working quickly enough to protect the rainforests.

3 The purple frog is unusual because ...
   a it sounds like another animal. **b** it can't move very quickly.

4 The purple frog was discovered ...
   a in 2003. **b** in 2009.

5 The scientist ...
   a doesn't think the frog can be saved. **b** wants people to help save the purple frog.

POST-LISTENING

12 Work with a partner. Look at the photos. What types of problems connected to climate change can you see?

North America

Brazil

Pakistan

13 Think about the plants and animals in the places in the photos and how climate change affects them. Make notes of your ideas.

14 Present your ideas to the class.

DISCUSSION

SYNTHESIZING

15 Work with a partner. Use ideas from Listening 1 and Listening 2 to discuss the following questions.

1 Have you ever been personally affected by global warming? How?
2 What could be some other negative results of global warming, for individuals, for countries and for the world?

PLUS

SPEAKING

CRITICAL THINKING

At the end of this unit, you are going to do the speaking task below.

Give a presentation about climate change.

UNDERSTAND

1 Work with a partner. You are going to study climate change in the Arctic. What effect has climate change had on weather in the Arctic? Make a list of how problems with the weather in the Arctic could affect people, animals and the environment.

2 Work with a partner. Read the problems connected to climate change in the Arctic. Did you and your partner have the same ideas?

Evaluating effects

SKILLS

Using a cause-effect chain can help you to organize your thoughts before a speaking task. Use your cause-effect chain to evaluate the possible effects of events or decisions. For example, the chain below shows that rising temperatures cause polar ice to melt.

Cause and effect is not the same thing as one thing happening after another. For example, if you wash your car and then it rains, washing the car did not cause it to rain.

EVALUATE

3 Decide which of the phrases in the box have a direct cause-and-effect relationship. Then, use the phrases to complete the cause-effect chain. Can any stages of the cause-effect chain repeat? If so, draw an arrow from the box that could cause something in the chain to occur again.

local people lose food sources ~~temperatures rise~~ polar bears and other animals lose sea ice to hunt from sea levels rise

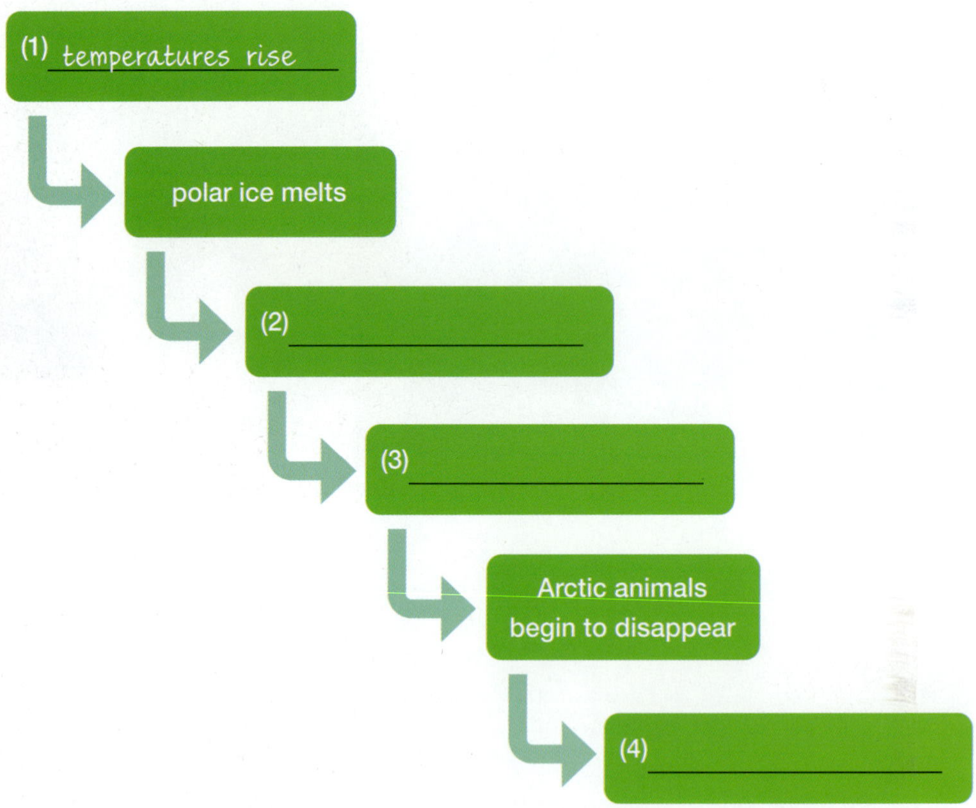

4 Work with a partner. How is the cause-effect chain useful? How would it help you if you were giving a presentation?

CREATE

5 Work with a partner. Create your own cause-effect chain for Africa, California or low-level lands. Use the information from the boxes below and your own ideas.

AFRICA

Some land areas will be under the sea.

Drought will stop farmers from growing food.

Shortage of clean water will help diseases spread.

By 2050, up to 600 million people won't be able to get drinking water.

Some areas may lose up to 60% of animal species.

Temperatures rise.

CALIFORNIA

People lose homes and jobs.

Heat waves occur.

Trees die.

Drought occurs.

Less water is on the land.

Wildfires occur.

Temperatures rise.

LOW-LEVEL LANDS (MALDIVES, THE FLORIDA COASTLINE)

Some people lose their home or country.

People have to find new homes or countries to live in.

Low-level land around the world floods.

Temperatures rise.

Land areas go under water.

Ice on land melts around the world.

Sea levels rise.

6 Can the cause-effect chain repeat? If so, draw an arrow from the box that could cause something in the chain to occur again.

PREPARATION FOR SPEAKING

LINKING WORDS TO EXPLAIN CAUSE AND EFFECT

SKILLS

You can use words to let a listener know that what comes next will be an explanation of the cause of something. Examples of linking words for causes are *because*, *because of* and *due to*.

More trees disappear **because** the changes in temperature stop the normal growth of the forest.

You can also use linking words to show that what comes next is the effect of something. Examples of effect linking words are *so*, *therefore*, *consequently* and *as a result*.

Another experiment showed that really humid weather changes how we work. **As a result,** it is more difficult to work and it's hard to pay attention.

Word order is important to help the listener know if a cause or an effect will follow. The linking word should come right before the cause or effect.

1 Label the sentences (a–b) in each pair (1–3) *cause* or *effect*.

1 a It is more difficult to work in high humidity. ___________
  b Our concentration drops. ___________

2 a People have more energy in sunny weather. ___________
  b They can get a lot done if the sun is shining. ___________

3 a There isn't enough water for people to drink. ___________
  b Some countries are very hot and don't get much rain. ___________

2 4.5 Listen and complete the sentences with the words and phrases you hear.

1 It is more difficult to work in high humidity, ___________ our concentration drops.
2 People have more energy in sunny weather. ___________ , they can get a lot done if the sun is shining.
3 Some countries are really hot and don't get much rain. ___________ , there isn't enough water for people to drink.

3 Work with a partner. Think of an effect for each sentence. Use *so*, *therefore*, *consequently* or *as a result* to show that an effect is coming next.

1 The rainfall was too heavy.
  Therefore the village flooded.
2 A new factory was built in the city.
  ____
3 Nowadays, more people are interested in global warming ...
  ____
4 Rainforests are getting smaller ...
  ____
5 I lost my passport ...
  ____
6 Communication is much easier nowadays ...
  ____

4 Choose four sentences from Exercise 3. Put the effect first and explain the causes. Use *because of*, *because* or *due to* to show that a cause is coming next.

The village flooded (effect) due to the heavy rainfall (cause).

1 ___________
2 ___________
3 ___________
4 ___________

PLUS

5 Compare your sentences with a partner.

6 Climate change is one effect of burning fossil fuels. Look at the pictures and try to understand the process.

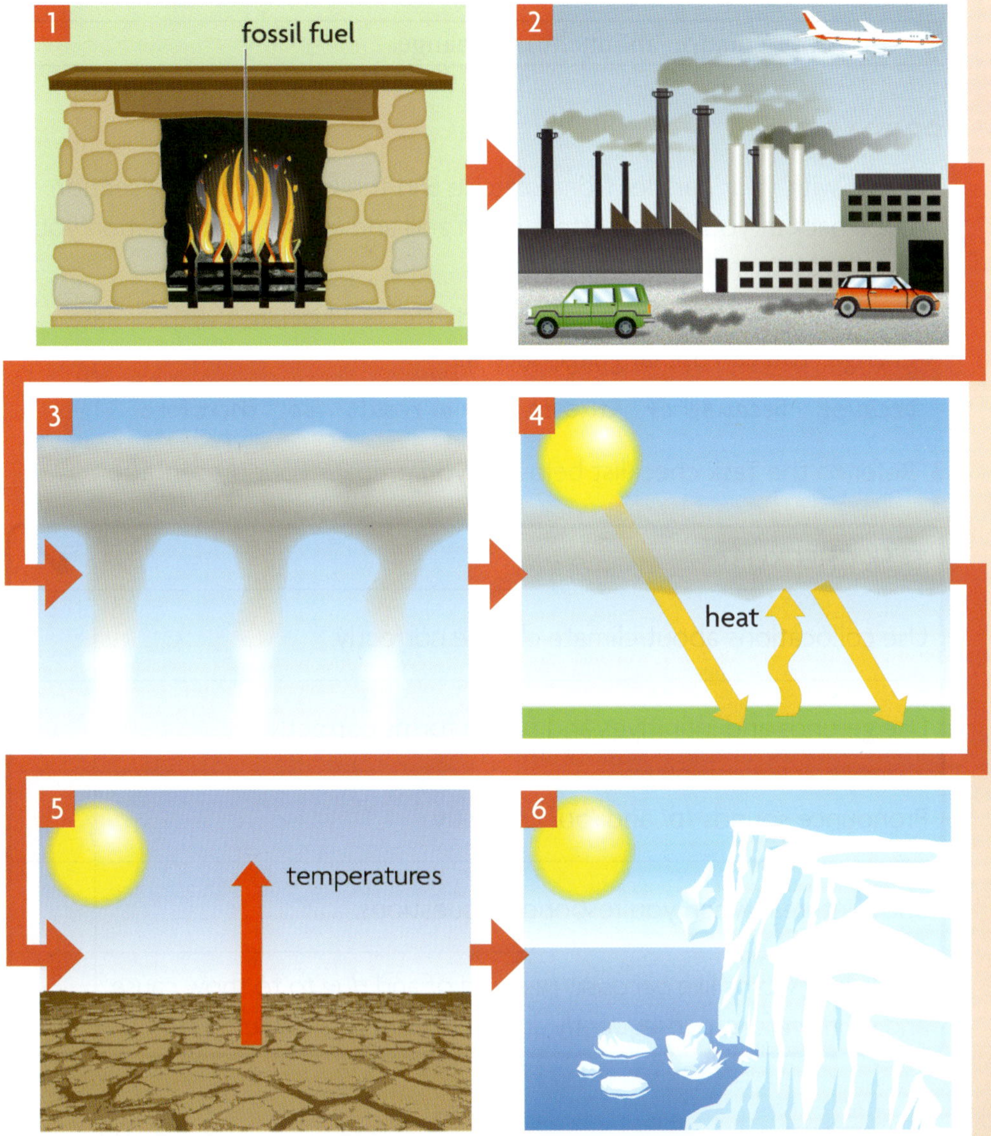

7 Work with a partner. Use the pictures in Exercise 6 and the words in the box to create a cause-effect chain to show how climate change can happen. Use a dictionary to help you.

burn	factory	gas(es)	heat	ice	melt	smoke	trap

8 Work with a partner. Describe the chain together. Use linking words from Exercises 3 and 4 to explain causes and effects.

SPEAKING TASK

Give a presentation about climate change.

PREPARE

1 Work with your partner from Exercise 6 in the Critical thinking section. Look back at your cause-effect chain and add any new information you would like to include.

2 Write phrases to describe causes and effects associated with climate change. You can use language such as:

because   because of   due to   as a result   so   therefore

3 Refer to the Task checklist below as you prepare your presentation.

TASK CHECKLIST	✔
Use collocations about climate change correctly.	
Use gerunds and infinitives and future forms correctly.	
Pronounce sounds /ɒ/ and /əʊ/ correctly.	
Show interest when you respond to questions.	
Use linking words like *because*, *because of* and *due to* to show cause and *so*, *therefore*, *consequently* and *as a result* to show effect.	

PRACTISE

4 Decide how you will present. Make sure you both say something. Practise your presentation with your partner.

PRESENT

5 Give your presentation about climate change to the rest of the class.

6 While listening to other pairs, take notes on questions that you have. Then ask questions at the end of each presentation. Together, talk about how to solve the problems.

OBJECTIVES REVIEW

1 Check your learning objectives for this unit. Write *3*, *2* or *1* for each objective.

3 = very well 2 = well 1 = not so well

I can …

watch and understand a video about the impact of oceans on climate.	____
predict ideas from research.	____
evaluate effects.	____
use gerunds and infinitives.	____
use future forms.	____
use linking words to explain cause and effect.	____
give a presentation about climate change.	____

2 Use the *Unlock* Digital Workbook for more practice with this unit's learning objectives.

UNLOCK ONLINE

WORDLIST

angry (adj)	discover (v) ⊙	prefer (v) ⊙
become (v) ⊙	dry (adj) ⊙	prevent (v) ⊙
believe (v) ⊙	energy (n) ⊙	rainforest (n)
carefully (adv) ⊙	forest fire (n)	save (v) ⊙
cool (adj)	global warming (n)	unusual (adj) ⊙
cut down (v)	humid (adj)	upset (adj)
disappear (v) ⊙	look after (v)	wildlife (n)

⊙ = high-frequency words in the Cambridge Academic Corpus

LEARNING OBJECTIVES	IN THIS UNIT YOU WILL ...
Watch and listen	watch and understand a video about a chess master playing against a computer.
Listening skills	listen for bias; listen for supporting opinions.
Critical thinking	build a strong argument.
Grammar	use the zero conditional and the first conditional; use adverbs of degree.
Speaking skills	emphasize a point; ask for and give clarification.
Speaking task	have a discussion about money in sport.

SPORTS AND COMPETITION

UNIT 5

UNLOCK YOUR KNOWLEDGE

Work with a partner. Look at the photo and answer the questions.

1 Which sport and event can you see in the photo? Is this sport popular in your country? Which sports are popular?

2 Do you prefer to play individual or team sports? Why?

3 Do you like to win? Is it more important to win a competition or just to play for fun?

PLUS

WATCH AND LISTEN

PREPARING TO WATCH

ACTIVATING YOUR KNOWLEDGE

1 Work with a partner. Answer the questions.

1 Can you name some popular board games?
2 Why do people like to play games?
3 How do people usually feel when they win or lose a game?

PREDICTING CONTENT

2 You are going to watch a video about a famous chess game. Decide which statements are true. Compare your answers with a partner.

1 You need to think a lot when you play chess.
2 Computers can play chess better than humans.
3 It doesn't take long to play a game of chess.

GLOSSARY

IBM (n) the name of an American technology company

genius (n) someone who is excellent at doing something; a very intelligent person

move (n) in a game like chess, a change of the position of one of the pieces, or a person's turn to play

trick (v) to make someone believe something that is not true

escape (v) to get away from a dangerous or bad situation

WHILE WATCHING

UNDERSTANDING MAIN IDEAS

3 Watch the video. Write *T* (true) or *F* (false) next to the statements below. Correct the false statements.

_____ 1 Humans began playing chess nearly 500 years ago.
_____ 2 Garry Kasparov played a famous chess match against a child.
_____ 3 A computer can only calculate numbers to play chess.
_____ 4 An engineer moved the chess pieces.
_____ 5 A genius like Kasparov can think about three moves a minute.

4 Watch again. Write the events in the correct column in the table.

a Garry Kasparov played the game very well.
b It seemed like the computer was thinking.
c The computer did not make a move for 15 minutes.
d In the end, the computer lost.
e The game took nearly four hours.
f Kasparov tried to trick the computer.

first game	second game

UNDERSTANDING DETAIL

5 Work with a partner. Circle the correct answers. Then, watch the video again and check your answers.

1 Where did humans begin playing chess?
a India b Russia
2 When did Garry Kasparov play a famous match?
a in the 1980s b in the 1990s
3 What is the computer's name?
a Big Blue b Deep Blue
4 How many moves can the computer think about in a second?
a 20 million b 200 million
5 What did Kasparov do at the end of the second game?
a he escaped b he lost

MAKING INFERENCES

6 Work with a partner. The speaker in the video says that 'to play chess well, you need many different skills'. Look at the skills in the box and decide which ones you need to be good at to play chess.

communication computer programming listening maths physical fitness planning teamwork thinking

DISCUSSION

7 Work in small groups. Discuss the questions.

1 What other games can humans play against computers?
2 Is it better to play games against a human or a computer? Why?
3 Are computers becoming more intelligent than humans? Give reasons.
4 How can computers help you learn to play and get better at games or sports?

LISTENING

LISTENING 1

PRONUNCIATION FOR LISTENING

SKILLS

Making corrections

When people speak, they sometimes make mistakes and correct themselves. If they correct themselves, they often emphasize the correct words. They do this with intonation and stress to make sure the people listening hear the change clearly.

OK, we're going to have a test tomorrow. Oh, sorry, I mean the day after tomorrow.

1 Underline the word that shows the correct information in the sentences.

1 The teacher's name isn't Mr Rosso. It's Mr Rosson.
2 I had a golf lesson, not a tennis lesson.
3 The match is at 6:00 tonight, not 6:30, so don't be late.
4 Yasmin doesn't do Drama classes; she does Gymnastics classes.
5 The competition will be in Colombia, not in Brazil.

2 5.1 Listen to the sentences in Exercise 1. Then answer the questions.

1 Which words does the speaker stress most strongly in each sentence?
2 Does the intonation go up or down at the end of the sentence?

3 Work with a partner. Take turns correcting the sentences by changing the underlined words to make them true, or true for you. Then read the sentences aloud to each other. Try to use the correct stress and intonation.

The most popular sport in my country isn't football. It's basketball.

1 The most popular sport in my country is basketball.

____

2 My favourite sport is bowling.

____

3 Formula One drivers race on motorbikes.

____

4 We use a football to play golf.

____

5 I study Sports Science.

____

PREPARING TO LISTEN

UNDERSTANDING KEY VOCABULARY

4 You are going to listen to a Sports Science student give a presentation about a project. Read the definitions. Then complete the sentences with the words in bold.

> **champion** (n) someone who wins a competition
> **compete** (v) to do an activity with others and try to do it better than they do
> **hit** (v) to touch something quickly and forcefully with the hand or an object
> **intelligent** (adj) able to understand and learn well
> **kick** (v) to hit someone or something with the foot
> **strong** (adj) physically powerful

1 Which person needs to have really __________ arms, a cricket player or a golfer? They both want the ball to go a long way.
2 Chess players are often __________ people. They need to think a lot as they play and plan their moves.
3 Eduardo likes to __________ against others in sports like cycling. He is really fast and usually wins his races.
4 Martina became the tennis __________ for our region. She beat all the other tennis players and got a medal as a prize.
5 In football, every player can __________ the ball with their feet, but can they use their hands sometimes?
6 In volleyball, can the players use their feet or can they only __________ the ball with their hands?

5 Work with a partner. Compare your answers in Exercise 4.

LISTENING FOR MAIN IDEAS

WHILE LISTENING

6 5.2 Listen to a Sports science student give a presentation about a project. Number the photos below in the order she talks about them.

a ☐

b ☐

c ☐

d ☐

TAKING NOTES ON DETAIL

7 5.2 Listen again. Complete the student's notes.

Unusual sports

- **Chess boxing:** chess – (1)__________ players need to think carefully
  boxing – strong boxers have to (2)__________ each other
  do two activities – first (3)__________ , next (4)__________
  benefit – both mental and physical activity
- **Urban golf:** use golf clubs and (5)__________ balls
  play in the (6)__________ , not on golf course
  advantages – don't need to go anywhere and don't need much (7)__________ to play
  disadvantage – might (8)__________ something if hit ball too hard
- **Sahara Marathon:** happens over (9)__________ days
  longest distance run in one day – 92 kilometres
  benefit – winner can say has won the (10)__________ race in world
- **Sepak takraw:** type of volleyball, players use different balls and use (11)__________ , knees, chest, or (12)__________
  started in (13)__________
  popular in Southeast Asia, Thailand, Indonesia
  benefit – gets children to play sports because played in (14)__________ in many countries

LISTENING FOR MAIN IDEAS

8 5.3 Listen to the excerpts from Listening 1. Cross out the mistake that the speaker makes in each sentence below. Then write the correct word or words above it.

1 In chess boxing, they begin with boxing and then switch.

2 For urban golf, you use golf clubs and a golf ball to play.

3 The Sahara Marathon happens over a week in Morocco.

4 Sepak takraw began in Indonesia and is very popular.

POST-LISTENING

9 5.3 Complete the sentences from Listening 1 with the phrases in the box. Then listen again and check.

no, not	or rather	sorry, I mean	well, actually

1 They start with boxing, ____________ chess.
2 You get clubs and a golf ball – ____________ , it's a soft tennis ball instead of a hard golf ball.
3 This race is held every year over a week ____________ over six days.
4 The sport began in Indonesia and it – ____________ Indonesia – it began in Malaysia.

10 Choose a popular sport. Write a sentence about the sport, but include a factual mistake in it.

____

____

11 Work with a partner. Take turns reading your sentence from Exercise 10 aloud. Then correct it using phrases from Exercise 9.

In football you need ten players in a team – well, actually, you need 11 players, 10 to play and a goalkeeper.

DISCUSSION

12 Work in small groups. Look at the notes in Exercise 7. Talk about which of the sports from the presentation you would like to watch or try. Why are you interested in that sport? Do you want to try it or just watch it? Why? Ask follow-up questions.

PLUS

LANGUAGE DEVELOPMENT

CONDITIONALS

GRAMMAR

The zero conditional and the first conditional

Use the zero conditional to talk about facts, habits and routine things that happen under certain conditions. Use the present simple in both the *if*-clause and the result clause.

if-clause | *result clause*

If you **play** urban golf, you **don't need** to go anywhere special.

Use the first conditional to talk about things that will happen under certain conditions in the future. Use the present simple in the *if*-clause and *will* / *won't* in the result clause. You can use other modal verbs in the result clause.

if-clause | *result clause*

If James **wins** the next race, he **will be** able to compete in the Olympics this year.

if-clause | *result clause*

If you **work** hard, you **might do** well in the competition.

1 Complete each sentence with a result clause. Put the words in brackets in the correct order, using the correct form of the verb.

Use the zero conditional

1 (the match ball / keep / they / to / get)
If a player scores three goals, ______________________________
______________________________.

2 (have to / you / the pitch / leave)
If you get a red card, ______________________________
______________________________.

3 (they / injured / get / often)
If athletes don't warm up properly, ______________________________
______________________________.

4 (game / win / you / the)
If you get the lowest score in golf, ______________________________
______________________________.

5 (three / you / points / get)
If you score from outside this line, ______________________________
______________________________.

Use the first conditional

6 (the / champions / be / they)
If my team wins the match on Saturday, ______________________________ .

7 (you / golf clubs / need / to buy)
If you decide to try urban golf, ______________________________ .

8 (have / more / you / strength)
If you start to lift weights, ______________________________ .

9 (she / be / successful)
If your friend has a trial for the volleyball team, ______________________________ .

10 (cancel / they / it)
If it rains hard before the game tomorrow, ______________________________ .

PLUS

2 Work with a partner. Check your answers from Exercise 1. Discuss any answers that are different.

3 Complete the conditional sentences (zero or first) about sports or activities that you do.

If I play my favourite sport, I always ask my brother to play, too.

1 If I play my favourite sport, ______________________________ .

2 If I have free time at weekends, ______________________________ .

3 If I get a chance to try a new sport next summer, ______________________________ .

4 If my friend wants to do something unusual this weekend, ______________________________ .

4 Work with a partner. Compare your sentences from Exercise 3. Ask follow-up questions.

ADVERBS OF DEGREE

GRAMMAR

Adverbs of degree can make other adverbs or adjectives stronger or weaker.

weak					strong
not very	*fairly*	*quite*	*pretty*	*very/really*	*extremely*

The runner was **not very** fast. (makes the adjective weaker)

Both teams played **extremely** well, but my team won in the end. (makes the adverb stronger)

The tickets for the match were **very/really** expensive, so I couldn't go. (makes the adjective stronger)

Use the adverb *too* to say that something is more than wanted or needed.

Tennis is **too** difficult. I don't like to play it.

5 Complete the sentences with an adverb of degree. In some items, more than one answer is possible. Then decide if the adverb of degree makes the adjective or adverb stronger (*S*) or weaker (*W*).

1 Football is ___very___ popular as a sport all over the world. ___S___
2 I don't go to see professional matches often because they are __________ expensive. _____
3 She played __________ badly – she didn't win any points at all! _____
4 Sophia is __________ competitive. In fact, this weekend she is running in two races. _____
5 Mehmet's __________ tired, but not that much. He's still going to play in the match this afternoon. _____
6 The coach said the team would arrive at six o'clock, but they arrived at ten to six, so they were __________ early. _____
7 The match starts in 10 minutes and it's on the other side of town – it's __________ late to go now. _____

PLUS

6 Work with a partner. Compare your answers.

7 Work with a partner. Ask and answer the questions.

1 What sports or activities can you do very well?
2 What sports or activities are you not very good at?
3 Are there any subjects or topics that you are extremely interested in? What are they?
4 When was the last time you arrived too late for an event?
5 What things do you find fairly boring in your job or studies?

LISTENING 2

PREPARING TO LISTEN

UNDERSTANDING KEY VOCABULARY

1 You are going to listen to a discussion about money in sports. Read the sentences (1–8). Then write the correct form of the words in bold next to the definitions (a–h).

1 Big tennis **competitions** like the Australian Open, the French Open and Wimbledon are held every year.
2 **Fans** from around the world come to watch their favourite tennis players compete against each other.
3 The **cost** of putting together and organizing these tennis matches is very high. Organizers have to pay a lot of money.
4 Organizers sometimes **charge** people a lot of money for tickets to a big sporting event.
5 Most athletes are not paid a **salary**, which people get when they have a full-time job.
6 Sometimes a company or a government will pay athletes money to **support** them and make sure they have enough money to train.
7 In football, the team that **scores** more goals wins the match.
8 The winner of the tennis match will get a **prize** of £600,000 and a trophy.

a ________ (n) something valuable that is given to someone who wins a game or has done good work
b ________ (v) to ask someone to pay for something, especially for an activity or a service
c ________ (v) to get points in a game or in a test
d ________ (n) the amount of money that you need to buy or do something
e ________ (n) the amount of money that you get from your job, usually paid every month
f ________ (n) someone who likes a famous person, sport, type of music, etc.
g ________ (v) to take care of someone by paying for his or her food, clothes, etc.
h ________ (n) an organized event in which people try to win by being the best, the fastest, etc.

PLUS

WHILE LISTENING

SKILLS

Listening for bias

Before listening, think about who is talking and why. Sometimes people are biased. They will have a reason to agree or disagree with something. For example, a business that is trying to get advertising might say it is OK to pay to have their name on a stadium. But a sports fan might want to have a stadium named after a famous athlete. So if you think about people and what they care about, this can give you information about what they might think before they speak. You can then listen for words that help you understand their opinions.

2 Andre and Ian will discuss if companies should pay athletes to train. Read the descriptions. Then decide who is most likely to have each opinion, *Ian* or *Andre*.

Ian: a long-time sports fan **Andre:** a former university football player

_______ 1 Obviously, athletes should be able to take money from companies for support.

_______ 2 Actually, seeing adverts everywhere at the Olympics is quite annoying.

LISTENING FOR BIAS

3 5.4 Listen to the discussion. Check your predictions in Exercise 2.

1 What bias does Ian, the fan, have?
2 What bias does Andre, the former sportsperson, have?

TAKING NOTES ON OPINION

4 5.4 Listen again. Complete the student's notes.

Athletes should be able to take money from companies to help with their training.

agree

- Reason: without the (1)_______ , athletes have no job
  Support: athletes can't live, work and pay for training; cost of coaching is really high
- Reason: athletes need good coaching
  Support: don't do well in competitions, lose chance to (2)_______ ; only (3)_______ % of Olympic athletes get money from companies
- Reason: a lot of countries can't pay the costs for (4)_______
  Support: more people can (5)_______
- Reason: good for everyone – athletes, (6)_______ , fans
  Support: everyone gets money or lower costs

disagree

- Reason: all athletes are interested in is making huge (7)_______ of money
  Support: more marketing than ever
- Reason: athletes are like (8)_______
  Support: get paid to wear companies' names on clothing; (9)_______ contracts
- Reason: athletes should represent their (10)_______
  Support: there would be less pressure to get money from a company
- Reason: all the money takes away from Olympics
  Support: see (11)_______ everywhere

POST-LISTENING

SKILLS

Supporting opinions

When speakers give an opinion, they need to support it. Without support, there is no reason why others should believe you. Support can be facts, examples, information from research, or what someone said. Not all information you find on the internet is correct, so be sure your support is true. You can get support from news, books, magazines, the internet or personal experiences.

Opinion only: *I think she's a great athlete.*

Opinion with support: *I think she's a great athlete because she won an Olympic gold medal.*

5 Work with a partner. Read the sentences from Listening 2. Is the speaker giving an opinion or giving information to support an opinion? Write *S* (support) or *O* (opinion).

1 It seems like the athletes are more interested in making money than in representing their countries. ______
2 Without all the help from companies, he might not have enough money to play tennis as his 'job'. ______
3 And actually, only about five percent of Olympic athletes get money from big companies to be in adverts. ______
4 I read that in the UK, the government pays the country's Olympic athletes to train, so there is less pressure there to get money from a company. ______

DISCUSSION

SYNTHESIZING

6 Work with a partner. Use ideas from Listening 1 and Listening 2 to discuss the following questions.

1 Why do some sports become popular internationally while others are only popular in certain countries?
2 Are any sports popular in your country but not internationally? What are they?
3 Do you think advertising and sponsorship should be allowed in sport? Which kinds of products should not be advertised? Explain your answers.

Novak Djokovic

SPEAKING

CRITICAL THINKING

At the end of this unit, you are going to do the speaking task below.

Have a discussion about money in sport. Discuss arguments for and against athletes being paid extremely large amounts of money.

SKILLS

Building a strong argument

When you try to persuade someone, it is important to make a well-supported argument with reasons and evidence – not just your opinion. Your reasons and evidence should be correct and believable.

It is also important to think about why people might disagree with your idea. You should try to understand the other side of an argument, to help you support your own argument.

REMEMBER

1 Work with a partner. Answer the questions.

1 What are some reasons for an athlete to participate in a big sports competition like the Olympics or the World Cup?

____

____

____

____

2 Why do companies want to support athletes at big competitions?

____

____

____

____

3 What are two reasons why some fans don't like the idea of companies supporting athletes?

____

____

____

____

APPLY

2 Read the arguments below. Do they have enough support to persuade someone to agree? Write *E* (enough) or *NE* (not enough).

1 Sports players have short careers, so they have to make as much money as possible when they are famous. ___________

2 Athletes become more professional when they get paid more. ___________

3 Sports are not really that important and so people should not be paid a lot to play them. ___________

4 Sports players create a lot of money for their teams and clubs, so they should be paid well. ___________

5 It takes years of hard work to become excellent at a sport – so players who have trained hard should be rewarded. ___________

6 Because of television, sports organizations get a lot of money. It is right that players have high salaries. ___________

3 Compare your ideas with a partner. Do you agree? Give reasons for your opinion.

SKILLS

Using a persuasion map

A persuasion map helps you organize your ideas about a point. It gives you a place to write reasons *for* a point (you agree with an idea) or *against* a point (you disagree with it). It also helps you organize support for your reasons (evidence for why your opinion is correct). Using a persuasion map can help you organize your ideas when you want to get others to agree with your point of view.

4 Work in a group of three or four. Read your role card on page 190 (Student A, Student B, Student C, Student D) to prepare for the speaking task at the end of this unit.

EVALUATE

5 After reading your role card in Exercise 4, decide if you (as the person in the role) are for or against the argument below. Then choose an option to complete the sentence in the box. Think about reasons why you might be for or against and write three reasons in the persuasion map.

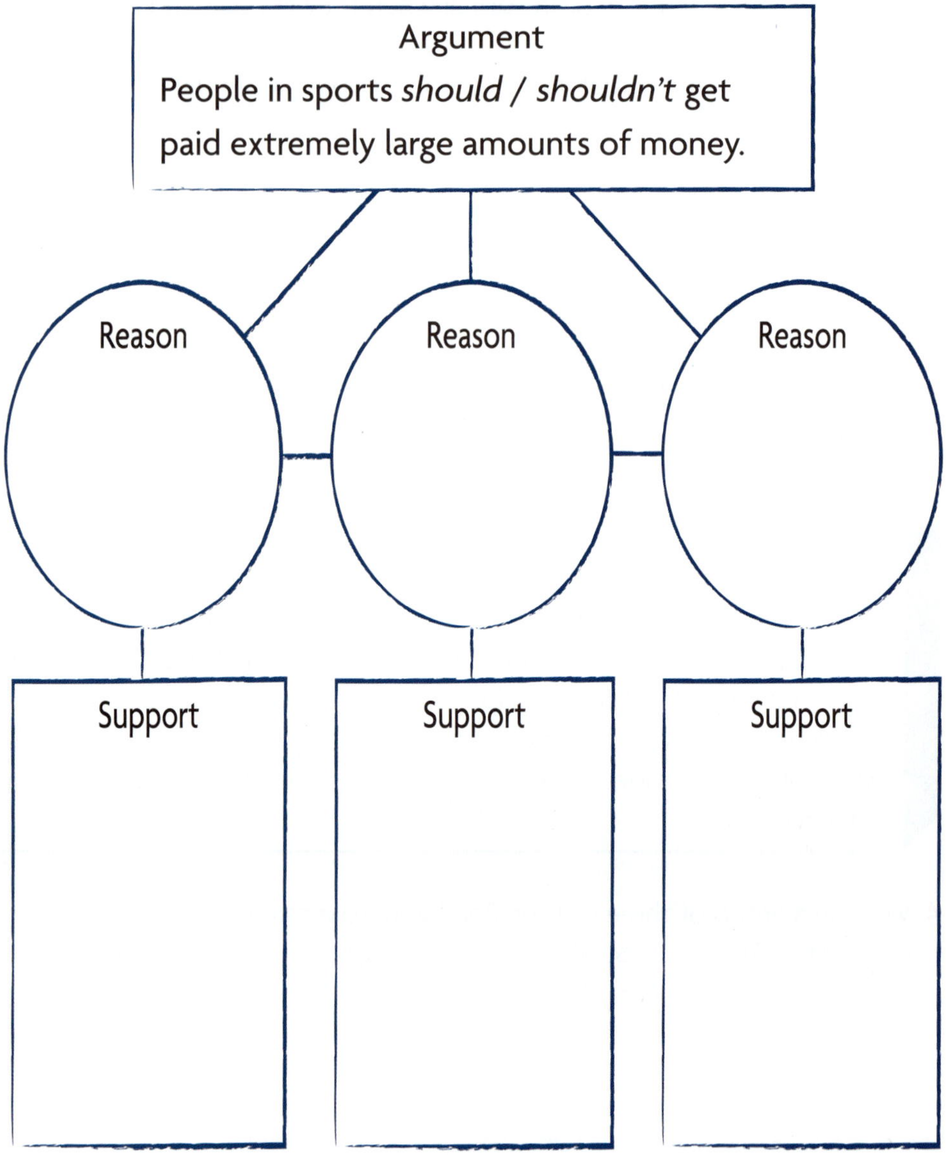

6 Now add one example or fact to support each reason. You can use information from Listening 2 or your own ideas. You will use this persuasion map for the speaking task at the end of this unit.

PREPARATION FOR SPEAKING

PRESENTING POINTS AND CLARIFYING STATEMENTS

SKILLS

Emphasizing a point

When you discuss a topic with others, you can use signal words to help you make a point strongly.

Of course, *obviously*, *actually* and *definitely* all signal to the listener that what comes next is going to be a point that you wish to emphasize.

And **actually,** a lot of people play tennis all over the world.

There are, **of course**, many professional athletes who take money from private companies to be in their adverts.

1 5.5 Listen to the sentences from Listening 2. Complete the sentences with the words in the box.

actually	definitely	of course

1 I think there is __________ more marketing and business in sport than ever before.
2 And __________, only about five percent of Olympic athletes get money from big companies to be in adverts.
3 And __________, the countries with lots of money can train their athletes very well.

2 Write sentences to give reasons and support either for or against the points you made in Exercises 5 and 6 in the Critical thinking section. Use *actually*, *definitely*, *obviously* or *of course* to emphasize your point in each sentence.

Sports fans actually like to see adverts with athletes in them.

a ______________________________
b ______________________________
c ______________________________
d ______________________________

3 Compare your sentences with a partner. Discuss your argument, reasons and support. Do you have similar ideas?

SKILLS

Asking for and giving clarification

Sometimes in a persuasive discussion, it isn't always clear what point someone is making.

If you don't understand what someone has said, you can use expressions like:

Sorry, I didn't follow what you said.
I'm afraid I didn't get that.
What do you mean by ... ?
I'm sorry, I don't understand.

If you want someone to explain more, you can use expressions like:

Could you give an example?
Can you give more detail?
Can you explain what you mean?

When someone asks you to clarify your point or idea, you can use these expressions:

Sorry, let me explain ...
To put it differently ...
In other words ...
Sure, for example ...

4 Work with a partner. Discuss the questions. Try to ask for and give clarification as you talk about your ideas.

1 The photo shows the sport of sepak takraw. Some rules of the game are that the tekong (the person who serves the ball) can't jump off the ground when she or he serves the ball and that you cannot shout at the other team. Why do you think the game has these rules?

2 Why do you think it's important to have rules in sports? Give support for your reasons. Are there any sport rules that you would change?

PLUS

5 An interviewer (I) is speaking to a sepak takraw competitor (C). Put the sentences in each part of the interview in the correct order, from 1–6.

Part 1

I: *What do you mean* by Tekong? ______

C: Yes, I thought we played well. We made a few silly mistakes, though. ______

C: That's the player who serves the ball during the match ... ______

I: Which mistakes did you make? *Can you give some more detail?* ______

C: Yes, sure. I thought that the ball went outside the court too much. Also, our Tekong jumped off the ground once or twice. ______

I: Did you enjoy the game? __1__

Part 2

C: Sure. One example is the excitement in the game from the players' amazing kicks ... ______

C: Definitely! I agree that it should be included. It's already in the Asian Games. ______

I: Can you give some examples of why people want to see this sport in the Olympics? ______

I: But even though it is in the Asian Games, can you explain more about why you support it? ______

C: Well, obviously, as a player I support it. But actually, even people who are not players want to see it in the Olympics. ______

I: I hear that people are trying to get sepak takraw included in the Olympics. Do you agree? ______

6 Work with a partner. Look at the questions in italics in Exercise 5, Part 1. What is another way to ask each of these questions of clarification?

7 Look at the interview in Exercise 5, Part 2. Underline the phrases that show ways of asking a person to explain more. Circle the words that show that the person is emphasizing a point.

8 Work with a partner. Compare your answers for Exercise 7.

9 Look at the phrases. Write *DU* (I don't understand) or *EM* (I want you to explain more).

1 Sorry, I didn't follow what you said. ________
2 Can you explain what you mean? ________
3 I'm afraid I didn't get that. ________
4 I'm sorry, but I don't understand. ________
5 Would you mind giving me some examples? ________

10 Work in a group of three. Follow the steps.

1 Choose a popular sport or activity.
2 Think of reasons why people would or wouldn't want to take part in it.
3 Think of support (facts or examples) for each reason you come up with.

11 Work with someone from another group. Follow the steps below.

1 Take turns explaining your ideas from Exercise 10 to each other. Try to use phrases to emphasize your points.

2 Ask each other for more information if you don't understand. Ask for support for reasons, if none are given.

SPEAKING TASK

Have a discussion about money in sport. Discuss reasons for and against athletes being paid extremely large amounts of money.

PREPARE

1 Work in your groups from Exercise 4 in the Critical thinking section. Read your role cards again on page 190 (Student A, Student B, Student C, Student D).

2 Look back at your persuasion map from Exercises 5 and 6 in the Critical thinking section. Add any new information.

3 Refer to the Task checklist below as you prepare for your panel discussion.

TASK CHECKLIST	✔
Use conditional forms correctly.	
Use key vocabulary to talk about sports.	
Ask for and give clarification using the correct language.	
Use signal words to clearly present your points.	
Give reasons and support (e.g. facts and examples) when presenting a point.	

DISCUSS

4 Have the discussion in your roles. Take turns stating your ideas individually before a general discussion. Student A should start. Remember to talk about your reasons for or against and give support for those reasons. Ask for clarification if you need to.

OBJECTIVES REVIEW

1 Check your learning objectives for this unit. Write *3*, *2* or *1* for each objective.

3 = very well   2 = well   1 = not so well

I can …

watch and understand a video about a chess master playing against a computer.	_____
listen for bias.	_____
listen for supporting opinions.	_____
build a strong argument.	_____
use the zero conditional and the first conditional.	_____
use adverbs of degree.	_____
emphasize a point.	_____
ask for and give clarification.	_____
have a discussion about money in sport.	_____

2 Use the *Unlock* Digital Workbook for more practice with this unit's learning objectives.

UNLOCK ONLINE

WORDLIST

champion (n)	fan (n) ⊙	salary (n)
charge (v) ⊙	hit (v) ⊙	score (v) ⊙
compete (v) ⊙	intelligent (adj) ⊙	strong (adj) ⊙
competition (n) ⊙	kick (v)	support (v) ⊙
cost (n) ⊙	prize (n)	

⊙ = high-frequency words in the Cambridge Academic Corpus

LEARNING OBJECTIVES	IN THIS UNIT YOU WILL ...
Watch and listen	watch and understand a video about food in coffee shops.
Listening skill	listen for numbers.
Critical thinking	identify solutions to problems.
Grammar	use comparatives and superlatives.
Speaking skill	give advice.
Speaking task	give advice to a failing business.

BUSINESS

UNIT 6

UNLOCK YOUR KNOWLEDGE

Work with a partner. Look at the photo and answer the questions.

1 What type of job do you think the person in the photo is doing?
2 Could you work in an office like this? Why / Why not?
3 What kind of job would you do if money wasn't important?
4 What are the advantages and disadvantages of working?

PLUS

WATCH AND LISTEN

PREPARING TO WATCH

ACTIVATING YOUR KNOWLEDGE

1 Work with a partner. Answer the questions.

1 Can you name some famous coffee companies?
2 Why do people like to go to coffee shops?
3 What are some things that coffee shops usually sell?

PREDICTING CONTENT

2 Work with a partner. You are going to watch a video about the coffee business. Discuss the statements. Do you agree or disagree?

1 Starbucks is the most popular coffee shop in the world.
2 People spend more money on coffee than on food in coffee shops.
3 People around the world prefer coffee from South America.

GLOSSARY

chain (n) a number of similar shops, restaurants, etc. owned by the same company

customer (n) a person or organization that buys things or services from a shop or business

headquarters (n) the main office of a company or organization

consultant (n) an expert in a particular subject who gives advice and information to businesses

model (n) an example of a way to organize and run a business

WHILE WATCHING

UNDERSTANDING DETAIL

3 Watch the video. Circle the correct answer.

1 ______ coffee shops are growing quickly in England.
  a Starbucks b Caffè Nero
2 Caffè Nero opened its first American shop in ______ .
  a New York b Boston
3 Gerry Ford ______ this coffee chain.
  a started b bought
4 Ford's coffee chain uses an ______ model.
  a American b Italian
5 Ford wants his customers to spend more money on ______ in his coffee shops.
  a food b coffee

UNDERSTANDING MAIN IDEAS

4 Watch again. Work with a partner and circle the correct answer.

1 Starbucks and *Caffè Nero / Costa Coffee* are two of the biggest coffee chains in the world.
2 Caffè Nero is *a British / an Italian* company.
3 30% of its sales are in *food / drinks*.
4 Caffè Nero is always busy for *lunch / dinner*.
5 A food consultant helps the company at its *coffee shops / headquarters*.
6 It is important to the company to sell *cheap / quality* food and coffee.

5 Work with a partner. Choose the best summary for the main idea of the video.

a Gerry Ford tries to sell sandwiches and biscuits that people will like.
b Gerry Ford's company has a successful business model.
c Gerry Ford's company doesn't try to copy other big coffee chains.

MAKING INFERENCES

6 Work with a partner. Why do you think it is important to give American customers Americanized food?

DISCUSSION

7 Work with a partner or in small groups. Discuss the questions.

1 What are the most popular coffee chains in your city or country?
2 What do coffee chains like Starbucks have in common?
3 Besides food and coffee, what are some other important things for coffee shop customers?

8 Imagine that you are working for Gerry Ford. Can you think of some new ideas to get customers to spend more money in his coffee shops? Share your ideas with the class.

LISTENING

LISTENING 1

PREPARING TO LISTEN

UNDERSTANDING KEY VOCABULARY

1 Read the definitions. Then complete the sentences with the correct form of the words in bold.

break (n) a pause in an activity for a short time
colleague (n) someone who works with you
earn (v) to get money from doing work
profit (n) money that you make from selling goods or services for more than they cost to make or provide
project (n) a piece of work that is for a particular purpose or a detailed study of a topic
spend time (phr) to use time to do something
waste time (phr) to use time badly

1 I don't __________ much money. My job doesn't pay very much and it is only part-time.
2 I was talking with some people at the office when another __________ came by and reminded us of a meeting with the boss.
3 Isabel __________ planning her tasks at the beginning of every workday because she wants to use her time well.
4 Looking at silly cat videos on the internet at work __________ that your company is paying you for.
5 Taryn's fashion company makes a big __________ . She doesn't pay much money for the materials or for the work to make the clothes and she sells them for a higher price.
6 At university I had to study and do a lot of library research on a __________ for my engineering course.
7 At 12:00 pm, all the workers took a __________ for lunch.

PRONUNCIATION FOR LISTENING

SKILLS

Pronouncing numbers

The way a number is pronounced may be different if the number is used in maths, science or banking.

Fractions: You may hear *a* or *one* in front of a fraction:

½ is *a half* or *one half*; ⅓ is *a third* or *one third*, etc.

Decimals: You may hear the word *point* in decimals. For example:

0.27 is *nought point twenty-seven* or *nought point two seven*.

Note: When *0* is in a longer set of information, say *zero*:

0044 1789 830 → *zero zero four four …*

Percentages: *%* is pronounced *percent* and is read directly after the number. For example:

27% is *twenty-seven percent*.

2 You are going to listen to a business student speak about a project that includes different numbers. Work with a partner. Say the numbers aloud.

1 48%
2 ½
3 ⅕
4 31.5
5 103
6 1,540
7 6,001
8 0.01

3 6.1 Listen to the numbers in Exercise 2 and repeat.

WHILE LISTENING

SKILLS

Listening for numbers

Numbers are difficult to hear if they are said quickly or if they are very long. You need to understand the numbers but also any words related to them, e.g. *percent* and *point*. Practise listening to and writing numbers as much as you can.

TAKING NOTES ON DETAIL

4 6.2 Listen to a conversation between a university professor and a student about her project. Complete Alika's notes on the outline of her research. Listen for numbers and words related to numbers.

How people waste time at work

- Internet and online use: almost (1) __________ of all workers wasted time surfing internet or writing personal (2) __________
- (3) __________ % spent time talking to colleagues
- (4) __________ % took longer coffee and lunch breaks
- 5% texting friends

Why people waste time at work

- ½ not happy in their (5) __________
- ⅓ thought they didn't (6) __________ a good enough salary
- not enough money for holidays and nice (7) __________
- (8) __________ % have to work too many hours

Effects on companies

- Workers don't work hard; productivity goes down, so company makes less money than it wanted to and can't pay workers higher (9) __________

5 6.2 Listen again. Write *T* (true) or *F* (false) next to the statements below. Then correct the false statements.

_____ 1 Alika has finished her research project.

_____ 2 She read more than 100 different reports.

_____ 3 Alika looked at why people like or dislike their jobs.

_____ 4 People waste time at work by surfing the internet, talking to other people and taking long breaks.

_____ 5 Alika says that productivity depends on how well workers do their jobs.

6 6.2 Listen again and look at the bar charts. Then write sentences showing how people wasted time at work (1–4) and the reasons for wasting time (5 and 6). Make sure your sentences match the data in the charts.

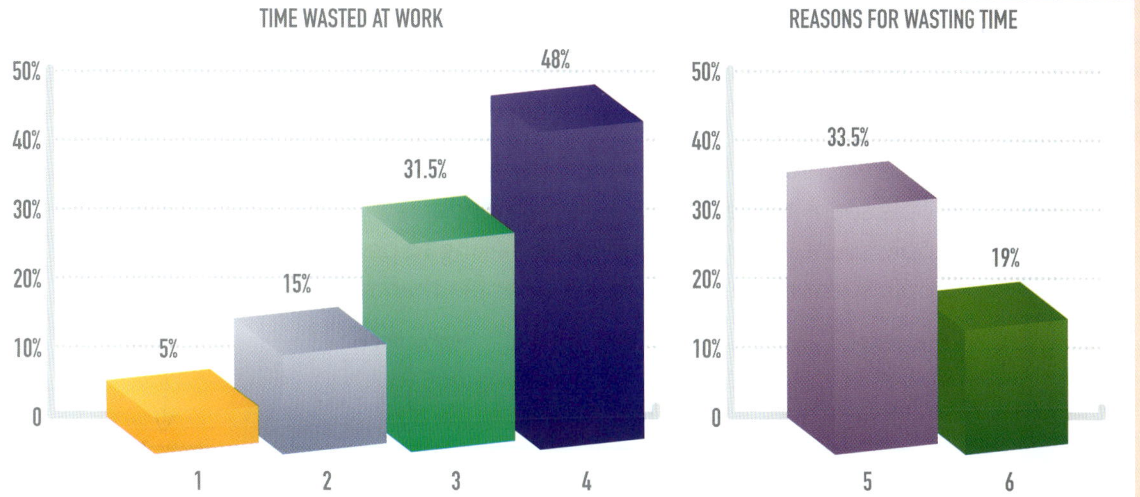

1 ____
2 ____
3 ____
4 ____
5 ____
6 ____

DISCUSSION

7 Work with a partner. Choose two ideas from the list that will stop people from wasting time at work. Why do you think these ideas will work?

1 Make sure everyone has a regular break.
2 Pay a very high salary.
3 Shout at people who waste time.
4 Give extra pay to people who work quickly.

8 Work with a partner. Do you agree or disagree with these sentences? Why / Why not?

1 Earning a lot of money is more important than having a fun job.
2 The most exciting kind of work is having your own business.
3 Younger people do not have enough experience to be good managers.
4 Older people with families don't work as hard as young, single people.
5 People who work the longest hours do the most work.
6 The best time to start working is after university.

LANGUAGE DEVELOPMENT

COMPARATIVES AND SUPERLATIVES

GRAMMAR

Comparing quantities

Use *more* (*than*), *less* (*than*), *the most* and *the least* to compare quantities.

1 People wasted **the most** time on the internet.
2 People spent **the least** time texting friends.
3 People spent **less** time texting **than** talking to people.
4 People spent **more** time talking to people **than** taking long breaks.

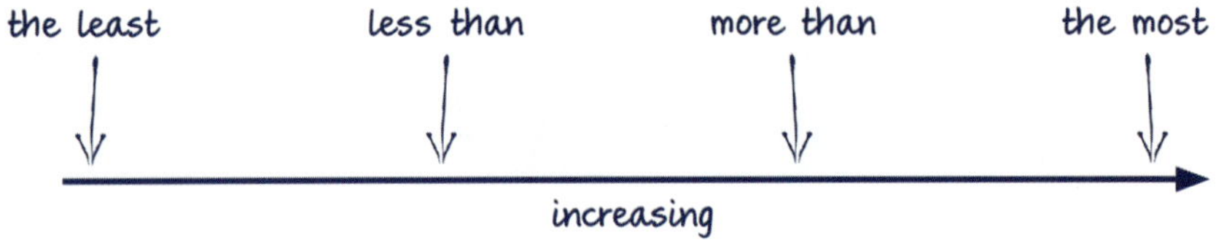

1 Use the information in the table to complete the sentences below.

time spent working at a desk	60%
time spent taking breaks	25%
time spent in meetings	10%
time spent on the phone	5%

1 People spent **the least** amount of time ______________ .
2 People spent **less** time ______________ **than** taking breaks.
3 People spent **the most** time ______________ .
4 People spent **more** time ______________ **than** in meetings.

2 Write three sentences using the words in bold in Exercise 1 and the information in the table below.

work-related reasons for not using time well	% of people
1 helping someone else with their work	54%
2 waiting for someone to finish their part of a project	42%
3 going to meetings	30%
4 filling in papers and forms	18%

1 People spent more time helping someone else with their work than going to meetings.
2 ______________
3 ______________
4 ______________

GRAMMAR

Comparative adjectives

Use comparative adjectives to compare two things.

For one-syllable adjectives, add *-er* and *than*. For one-syllable adjectives which end in one vowel and one consonant, double the last consonant and add *-er*. Do not double the consonant *w*.

old → older than   thin → thinner than   low → lower than

Sheila is **older than** her manager.

Use *more* before almost all adjectives with two or more syllables. *Less* is the opposite of *more*.

important → more important than / less important than

Having good colleagues is **more important than** having a good boss.

Money is **less important than** happiness.

For two-syllable adjectives ending in *-y*, remove the *-y* and add *-ier*.

happy → happier than

People who love their job are usually **happier than** people who don't.

Use *as* + adjective + *as* to say that two things are similar or the same.

Not as ... as means 'less than'.

My salary is **(not) as high as** yours.

Superlative adjectives

Use superlative adjectives to compare one thing or person against all others, or all the others in a group.

For one-syllable adjectives, add *the* and *-est*. For one-syllable adjectives which end in one vowel and one consonant, double the consonant and add *-est*. Do not double the consonant *w*.

young → the youngest   big → the biggest   low → the lowest

Muriel is **the youngest** person in the office.

Use *the most* or *the least* before almost all adjectives with two or more syllables.

experienced → the most experienced / the least experienced

I always listen to Lisa because she's **the most experienced** member of the team.

I don't say much in meetings because everyone knows I'm **the least experienced** person.

For two-syllable adjectives ending in *-y*, remove the *-y* and add *-iest*.

friendly → the friendliest

My colleague Evan is **the friendliest** person I know.

Some adjectives are irregular. Try to memorize their comparative and superlative forms.

good → better than → the best   bad → worse than → the worst

Working at home is **better than** working in an office.

What is **the worst** thing about your job?

3 Complete the sentences with the comparative or superlative form of the adjectives in brackets. Add words like *than*, *as* or *the*.

1 Is money ________________ (important) having an interesting job?
2 Is a job working inside as ________________ (good) a job working outside?
3 Do you think men are ________________ (bad) women at organizing things?
4 Is taking long breaks at work ________________ (serious) spending time on the internet?
5 Who is ________________ (funny) person you have worked with?
6 Which job do you think is ________________ (interesting)?

4 Work in groups of three. Ask and answer the questions in Exercise 3.

5 Look at the chart below. Write five sentences about the reasons employees give for being happy at work. What reason is most important? Which reasons are more important than others?

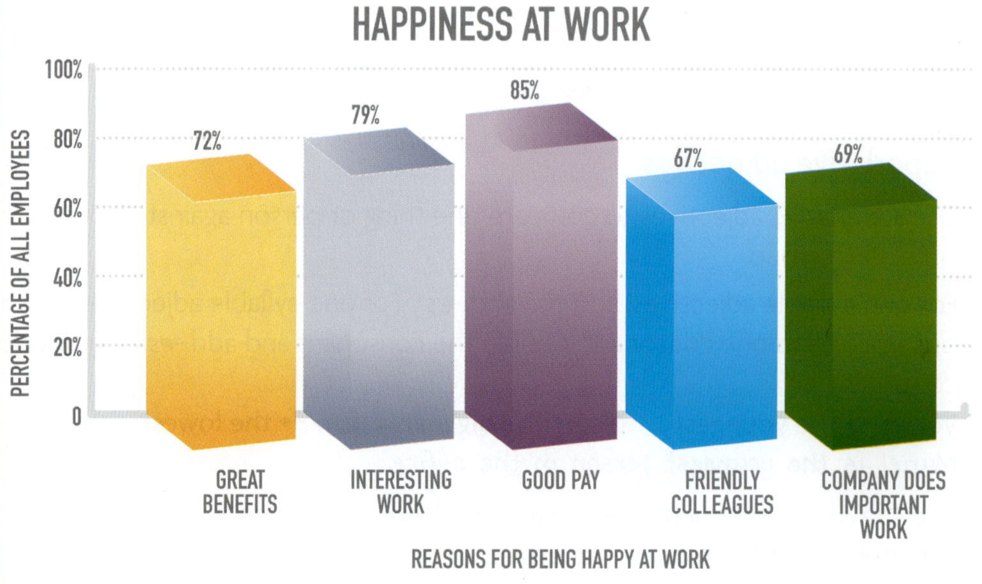

Source: http://www.workerhappiness.gov/reasonsbehappy

Good pay is the most important thing to employees.

1 ________________
2 ________________
3 ________________
4 ________________
5 ________________

PLUS

6 Work with a partner. Compare your answers in Exercise 5.

7 Work with a partner. Discuss the questions.

1 What do you think is the most important thing that makes other people happy at work?
2 Which reasons are more important to you? Which reasons are less important?
3 What else do you feel makes you happy at work? Is it more or less important than the reasons in the chart?

PHRASAL VERBS

VOCABULARY

Phrasal verbs are verbs with one or more *particles* (prepositions or adverbs). The verb and the particle(s) have a specific meaning when you use them together. This meaning can be very different from the meaning of the same verb on its own. Common particles in phrasal verbs include *up*, *down*, *back*, *out*, *on*, *off*, *in*, *by*, etc.

Verb: I **ran** for my bus. (= moved along faster than walking)
Phrasal verb: I **ran out** of time. (= used all of something so there is none left)

Look at the phrasal verbs and their definitions below.

find out	to get information about something, or to learn a fact for the first time
get by	to be able to live or deal with a situation with difficulty, usually by having just enough of something you need, such as money
look at	to think about a subject carefully so that you can make a decision about it
run out	to use all of something so that there is none left
take over	to replace someone or something
write down	to write something on a piece of paper so that you do not forget it

In some phrasal verbs, such as *write down*, it is possible to put other words between the verb and the particle.
I **wrote down** all the details. I **wrote** all the details **down**.

8 Look at the sentences. Underline all of the words which make phrasal verbs.

1 You wrote a lot of information down in my notebook.
2 I haven't finished yet – I ran out of time.
3 I wrote down some notes during the lecture.
4 Sandra took over from Mark as the project manager.
5 Amal found out a lot of information about the way people work.
6 Marta looked at how people use their time at work.
7 Faisal had just enough money to get by each month.

PLUS

9 Complete the sentences with the correct form of the phrasal verbs in the explanation box on page 135.

1 I've ________________ of money! I need to find a bank and use the cash machine.
2 Yumi ________________ that the company is planning to open a new office in Bangkok.
3 Can you ________________ this report and let me know if there are any mistakes?
4 We'll ________________ this year if we are careful with our money.
5 I'm sure I __________ the company's address __________ somewhere. Ah, here it is! 15 New Street!
6 I wonder who will ________________ as head of the company when Margaret retires.

10 Match the sentence halves. Use the phrasal verbs in bold to help you.

1 How do you **find** _c_
2 Would you like to **take** _____
3 Do you **write** _____
4 Have you ever **run** _____
5 Do you **look** _____
6 How can people **get** _____

a **out** of time to finish your work? What happened?
b **at** customer reviews before you buy something online? Why / Why not?
c **out** information about a company before a job interview?
d **by** if they lose their job? What advice would you give them?
e **down** people's phone numbers or put them straight into your phone?
f **over** someone's job if they lost it? Why / Why not?

11 Work with a partner. Ask and answer the questions in Exercise 10.

LISTENING 2

PREPARING TO LISTEN

UNDERSTANDING KEY VOCABULARY

1 Read the definitions. Then complete the sentences with the correct form of the words in bold.

careless (adj) done, made or said without paying attention
customer (n) someone who buys goods or services from a business
goal (n) something you want to do successfully in the future
messy (adj) untidy or dirty
skill (n) the ability to do an activity or job well
strength (n) a good quality
stress (n) feelings of worry caused by problems
weakness (n) a quality that is not good

1 My business __________ for next year is to build a new factory.
2 I share an office with a colleague, so we both make sure our desks are not __________ . It would be hard to work if things were not neat and clean.
3 The business was failing, so the owners looked for some __________ in their business plan. They wanted to find out what the problem was so they could fix it.
4 Understanding a foreign language is an important __________ in business these days.
5 The salesperson was very pleased when the __________ put in a large order. It was a successful day for the business.
6 When you go for a job interview, you should talk about your __________ to show the interviewer you are the best person to hire.
7 I was trying to work quickly and without thinking I made a __________ mistake. I ruined my entire project when I pressed the wrong button.
8 Ruining my project made me feel a lot of __________ . I had to do yoga after work to relax.

PLUS

USING YOUR KNOWLEDGE

2 You are going to listen to a conversation between Joe, a business consultant and Sam, a business owner. Work with a partner. Discuss the questions.

1 Look at the photo. Which person is the consultant? Give reasons.
2 Why would a business owner need advice from a consultant?
3 What skills do you think you need to be a business consultant? Do you think you would be good at it? Why / Why not?

WHILE LISTENING

TAKING NOTES ON DETAIL

3 6.3 Listen to the conversation. Complete Sam's notes about advice that the consultant gives him.

Advice for business

Problem: Workers are not (1)________ at work – they don't work hard
Solutions: (2)____________ once a month
(3)____________ a brighter colour
Result: Workers will be happier, work harder

Problem: Need to cut costs; spending too much money
Solution: Use less electricity; (4)____________ parts
Result: Make a better (5)________

Problem: Having trouble reaching new customers
Solution: Add (6)____________
Result: Get new customers

Problem: Old and messy website
Solution: Hire a (7)____________
Colour important: Colour can make the website (8)________
Colour can prevent customers from leaving the website before buying things
Website needs to look (9)________ and (10)________ to use
Result: Get more online sales

4 6.4 Listen to the first part of the conversation again. Number the phrases in the order you hear them.

a Was it useful ____
b Exactly! But there are things you think will cause you to lose money ____
c Oh, yes ____
d Well, when we looked at the company's strengths and weaknesses ____
e What is making you stressed about that ____
f Useful ... Yeah, it was ____

LISTENING FOR REACTION

5 Work with a partner. Decide which of the sentences in Exercise 4 look like statements and which sentences look like questions.

6 6.5 Listen to a sentence from Exercise 4. Does it sound like a statement or a question? Why?

7 6.6 Listen to the sentences in Exercise 4 again and repeat.

POST-LISTENING

MAKING INFERENCES

8 Work with a partner. Use the notes from Exercise 3 to answer the questions.

1 What do you think Sam and the consultant discussed in their meeting before this one? How do you know?
2 Do you think Sam feels positive or negative about their next meeting? Why?

DISCUSSION

SYNTHESIZING

9 Work with a partner. Use ideas from Listening 1 and Listening 2 to answer the following questions.

1 What types of advice can a business get from a consultant?
2 What do you think is the most important thing for a business to do in order to be successful?
3 If the workers in your business were not working as hard as you expected, what steps would you take?

PLUS

SPEAKING

CRITICAL THINKING

At the end of this unit, you are going to do the speaking task below.

Give advice to a failing business.

SKILLS

Identifying solutions to problems

To solve a problem, think about the reasons for the problem. What are possible solutions? What are the possible results? Which solutions will work? Use a problem and solution table to help you organize your ideas when you give advice about a problem.

REMEMBER

1 Work with a partner. What advice does the consultant give to the business owner in Listening 2? Match the possible solutions from the box (a–d) to the problems in the table (1–4).

- a Turn off the lights and computers at the end of the day; find cheaper parts for the products you make.
- b Add online sales.
- c ~~Organize social events and paint the office walls brighter colours.~~
- d Hire a professional web designer to create a well-organized website that is easier to use.

problems	possible solutions	possible results
The employees are unhappy and don't work hard.	→ 1 ___c___ →	Employees will be happier and work harder.
The company spends too much money on electricity and parts for the products they make.	→ 2 ______ →	
The business isn't getting new customers.	→ 3 ______ →	
The business has an old, messy website.	→ 4 ______ →	

2 Work with your partner from Exercise 1. Look back at your notes from Listening 2, Exercise 3 and complete the *possible results* column in the table.

3 Work with a partner. Choose one of the businesses below. You will discuss this business in the speaking task at the end of this unit.

ANALYZE

THE WAKE-UP CAFÉ

A small coffee shop just opened in a business area of a big city. The shop is open from 12 pm to 5 pm every day. The shop has no tables or chairs, because the owner wants people to leave after they buy their coffee. The owner also buys expensive coffee beans, because they are the most popular kind of coffee bean in the city. However, the owner complains that he is not getting enough customers and he is losing a lot of money very quickly. He might have to close the business next month if he keeps losing money and if more customers don't start coming into the shop.

DELIVERY RABBIT

A delivery company in a big city is not getting enough customers. Customers complain that the website is ugly and too hard to use, so they give up and choose other delivery companies. They also say that the deliveries are always late. The business has one delivery person who rides a bike. The business is losing a lot of money and might have to close if it doesn't get more customers soon.

FRESH FOOD MARKET

A small supermarket in a small town is losing a lot of money. Customers complain that it is too dirty and that the food is never fresh. Another small supermarket opened recently and is taking all of Fresh Food Market's customers. If it doesn't get its customers back, it will close next month.

4 Work with your partner from Exercise 3. Think about the business you chose. Write three or four possible problems in the problem and solution table.

business name: ______________________

problems		possible solutions		possible results
1	→		→	
2	→		→	
3	→		→	
4	→		→	

EVALUATE

5 Use the advice from Listening 1 and Listening 2 and your own ideas to think of solutions and their possible results. Add your ideas to the problem and solution table in Exercise 4.

PREPARATION FOR SPEAKING

GIVING ADVICE

SKILLS

You can use certain phrases to introduce advice at the beginning of a sentence. The second part of the sentence gives advice.

If you want to sell more, you should start by trying to improve your advertising.

Here are some key phrases you can use to introduce advice:

I think you should ...
Be careful not to ...
Why don't you ... ?
If I were you, I would ...
If you want to ... , you should ...

PLUS

1 Work with a partner. Look at the picture of a shop. Think of reasons why the shop might be having trouble with its business.

2 Work with a partner. Complete the sentences to give advice to the business in Exercise 1.

1 If I were you, I would ...

____ .

2 I think you should ...

____ .

3 If you want to do better, you should ...

____ .

4 Be careful not to ...

____ .

5 You should try (not) to ...

____ .

3 Read a conversation between the owner of Marco's Guitar & Café and his business consultant. Underline the advice that the consultant gives. There is also one piece of inferred advice (advice that you can guess because of information you have). What is it?

Consultant:	I think you should try to improve your shop.
Business owner:	Oh. Can you give an example of how?
Consultant:	Yes. I don't want to upset you, but your shop doesn't seem very attractive at the moment. It's a little messy in some places.
Business owner:	OK. I see what you're saying. I'll work on that and make the shop cleaner and tidier.
Consultant:	And if you want to bring in more customers, you need to have a more interesting front window.
Business owner:	Do I? That's not really one of my strengths.
Consultant:	I know it's difficult. I think you should hire a window designer. Then at least you know it will look nice.
Business owner:	OK, great. I appreciate all of your advice.

4 Work with a partner. Turn to page 190 and decide who is Student A and who is Student B. Then follow the instructions.

5 Work in a group of three. Imagine you are business consultants. Make a list of ten dos and don'ts for small businesses.

6 Work with a new partner. Compare your lists from Exercise 5. Create a new list with your ten best ideas.

SPEAKING TASK

Give advice to a failing business.

PREPARE

1 Look back at the business you chose and the problem and solution table on page 141 in the Critical thinking section. Add any new information.

2 Write a sentence to introduce advice for each problem in the table. Use your notes in the *possible solutions* column and language from the Preparation for speaking section.

1 ______________________________

2 ______________________________

3 ______________________________

4 ______________________________

3 Refer to the Task checklist below as you prepare for your discussion.

TASK CHECKLIST	✔
Say numbers correctly.	
Use comparatives and superlatives correctly.	
Use phrasal verbs correctly.	
Identify solutions to problems.	
Use phrases for giving advice.	

DISCUSS

4 Work with a partner who chose a different business in Exercise 3 of the Critical thinking section. Follow the steps below.

1 **Student A:** You are the owner of the business that Student B (the consultant) chose. Read the case study on page 141 for the business that Student B will give advice for.
2 **Student B:** Give advice to Student A on how he or she can solve the problems for the business. Describe possible results for each solution.
3 **Student A:** Take notes on Student B's advice. Which piece of advice do you think will be the most helpful? Why?
4 Switch roles and repeat.

OBJECTIVES REVIEW

1 Check your learning objectives for this unit. Write *3*, *2* or *1* for each objective.

3 = very well   2 = well   1 = not so well

I can ...

watch and understand a video about food in coffee shops.	_____
listen for numbers.	_____
identify solutions to problems.	_____
use comparatives and superlatives.	_____
give advice.	_____
give advice to a failing business.	_____

2 Use the *Unlock* Digital Workbook for more practice with this unit's learning objectives.

UNLOCK ONLINE

WORDLIST

break (n) ⊙	goal (n) ⊙	spend time (phr)
careless (adj)	look at (phr v)	strength (n) ⊙
colleague (n)	messy (adj)	stress (n) ⊙
customer (n) ⊙	profit (n) ⊙	take over (phr v)
earn (v) ⊙	project (n) ⊙	waste time (phr)
find out (phr v)	run out (phr v)	weakness (n) ⊙
get by (phr v)	skill (n) ⊙	write down (phr v)

⊙ = high-frequency words in the Cambridge Academic Corpus

LEARNING OBJECTIVES	IN THIS UNIT YOU WILL ...
Watch and listen	watch and understand a video about art made from rubbish in the sea.
Listening skill	listen for attitude.
Critical thinking	evaluate the importance of information.
Grammar	use the past continuous and the past simple.
Speaking skills	use correct time order; give examples and details.
Speaking task	give a presentation about a remarkable person and his or her work.

PEOPLE UNIT 7

UNLOCK YOUR KNOWLEDGE

Work with a partner. Look at the photo and answer the questions.

1 Some people are extraordinary. They do very special, unusual or strange things. Do you know anyone extraordinary? Who is it? What does he or she do?
2 Why is the person in the photo extraordinary? What kind of personality do extraordinary people have?
3 What extraordinary thing would you like to do?

PLUS

WATCH AND LISTEN

PREPARING TO WATCH

ACTIVATING YOUR KNOWLEDGE

1 Work with a partner. Answer the questions.

1 Where in the world is Kenya?
2 What ocean is to the east of Kenya?
3 What can you find on a beach?

PREDICTING CONTENT FROM VISUALS

2 Work with a partner. Look at the photos from the video and read the newspaper headline. Then answer the questions.

> **Kiwayu people earn money from the beach**

1 What can you see on the beach?
2 What are the people doing in the photos?
3 How do you think the people of Kiwayu Island make money?

GLOSSARY

isolated (adj) very far from other places
trash (US n) the things you throw away because you do not want them; rubbish
wash up (phr v) to move naturally from the water to the beach
flip-flop (n) a kind of open shoe that people often wear at the beach
ornament (n) an object that decorates a home or garden

WHILE WATCHING

UNDERSTANDING MAIN IDEAS

3 Watch the video. Circle the correct answer.

1 There *are / are not* a lot of tourists on the beaches of Kiwayu Island.
2 The people who live there seem *connected to / isolated from* the rest of the world.
3 People pick up rubbish on the beach *weekly / daily* to earn a living.
4 People turn the rubbish into *flip-flops / art*.
5 They *make / don't make* money from the tourists.
6 They send *some / most* of their ornaments to Nairobi, Kenya.
7 These ornaments are sold to shops around the *country / world*.

UNDERSTANDING DETAIL

4 Watch again. Work with a partner. Match the questions (1–8) to the answers (a–h).

1 Who goes to the beach to pick up rubbish?	a flip-flops
2 What do people collect on the beach?	b some of their children
3 Where do they take the flip-flops to?	c houses
4 Who turns the rubbish into ornaments?	d artists and craftsmen
5 What do the people of Kiwayu make?	e Kiwayu women
6 Where do people sell the ornaments?	f money
7 What did Kiwayu people not have before?	g on the internet
8 Who couldn't go to school before?	h their villages in Kiwayu

MAKING INFERENCES

5 Work with a partner. Why does the woman in the video say that education is the most important thing? Circle the best reason.

a Children can learn to pick up plastic and other rubbish.
b Staying at home on an island is boring to children.
c Children can have a better future.

DISCUSSION

6 Work with a partner. Discuss the questions.

1 How can we stop people from putting rubbish into the oceans?
2 Do you think turning rubbish into art is a good idea? Why / Why not?
3 What do artists and craftsmen in your country make for tourists?

7 Work in small groups. Imagine you are artists in Kiwayu. Look at the kinds of things which wash up on beaches in the box below. What could you make from each one?

bottle tops	boxes	glass bottles	paper bags
plastic bags	plastic cups	tyres	drink cans

LISTENING

LISTENING 1

PREPARING TO LISTEN

UNDERSTANDING KEY VOCABULARY

1 You are going to listen to a student presentation about creative people and the things they make. Read the sentences (1–8). Then choose the best definitions (a or b) for the words in bold.

1 I like the **design** of the new building in town. It has space for business as well as for relaxation.
  a the way something is planned and made
  b the parts of something that are needed
2 The 'spork' is a great example of **simple** design – just a fork at one end and a spoon at the other. Nothing else.
  a made without extra things that are not needed
  b produced in large quantities and cheap to buy
3 Modern computers are very **complicated** machines, but they are very easy to use.
  a having a lot of different pieces, in a way that is difficult to understand
  b worth a lot of money because the parts are very expensive
4 Salt has many **uses**. It can be used to cook and clean and it even has medical uses.
  a things you must or should have
  b ways in which something is used
5 Sara's new painting was so beautiful that she won a prize for her **achievement** in art.
  a money you receive for doing a job or winning a competition
  b something good and successful that you do, usually by working hard
6 Each part of your office chair has a **purpose**. The armrests on your chair hold up your arms so that your wrists are comfortable when you type.
  a the way something is made
  b why you do something or why something exists
7 When you give a presentation, you should have a few main **points**, like why something is important or how something helps people.
  a opinions, facts or ideas that are said or written
  b special computer software used for showing information on a screen
8 What do you think is the best **invention** made by someone trying to solve a problem – the phone, the computer or the internet?
  a something made for the first time
  b a piece of technology used for communication

2 Work with a partner. Discuss the questions.

1 What do you know about the following inventors: Leonardo da Vinci, Thomas Edison and Grace Hopper?
2 Who are some inventors and designers that you know of? What were their inventions or designs?
3 How did their inventions or designs change lives?

USING YOUR KNOWLEDGE

WHILE LISTENING

LISTENING FOR MAIN IDEAS

3 7.1 Listen and label the photos with the correct objects and people. One person is used twice.

object	person
hand dryer	Sir James Dyson
Egg chair	Sir Jonathan Ive
wheelbarrow	Arne Jacobsen
iPhone	

a

____

____

b

____

____

c

____

____

d

____

____

TAKING NOTES ON DETAIL

4 7.1 Read the student's notes and complete the information. Listen again and check your answers. Then compare your answers with a partner.

inventor/designer and interesting points	inventions/designs and achievements	why the person is important
Arne Jacobsen Hard worker, liked to joke, (1) ________ relaxed him	Chair: (2) ________ and neat design, his designs still used today → he worked to make them perfect	Was famous for (3) ________, simple designs of furniture and buildings; he thought about the (4) ________ his designs would serve for people
Sir James Dyson Studied (5) ________ & Design and Engineering; still interested in art – made waterfall with water going up, not down	Inventions include: wheelbarrow with round wheel, hand dryer, vacuum cleaner Supports education, research and gives money so (6) ________ will become inventors, too	Inventions made to solve (7) ________ Gets ideas because he sees things that can work better Dyson is still (8) ________ new things
Sir Jonathan Ive Made Knight Commander of the British Empire in 2012 Hardworking and (9) ________	Designed many products for Apple, which are (10) ________, clean and slim	Ive has won a lot of (11) ________ for his designs You can see his work in museums

DISCUSSION

5 Work in small groups. Discuss the questions.

1 Which of the three inventors or designers do you think is the most interesting? Why?
2 How do designers and inventors help improve life for people?
3 What inventions would you like to see in the next 20 years?

PLUS

LANGUAGE DEVELOPMENT

ADJECTIVE ENDINGS *-ED* AND *-ING*

VOCABULARY

Many adjectives end in *-ed* or *-ing*. Some can have both endings. These endings change the meaning of the adjective.

Adjectives that end in *-ed* describe what people feel as a result of something.
Sarah is **interested** in the inventor Thomas Edison.
I get **bored** when my internet connection isn't working.

Adjectives that end in *-ing* describe the reason for a feeling.
Stories about accidental inventions, like Post-it Notes®, are really **interesting**.
Stories about really simple inventions, like drinking straws, are pretty **boring**.

You can often change a word to an adjective by adding *-ed* or *-ing*.
relax (v) → **relaxed** (adj) / **relaxing** (adj)
surprise (n/v) → **surprised** (adj) / **surprising** (adj)
(Note: Remove the final *-e* in *surprise*.)

1 Look at the sentences from Listening 1. Underline the adjectives.

1 It's an interesting design.
2 He found painting to be relaxing.
3 He got frustrated and worked to improve it.
4 But he is also interested in supporting education.

2 Compare the two sentences (a and b) in the pairs of sentences (1–6). Circle the word that the adjective describes in each sentence.

1 a The news was surprising.
  b I was surprised by the news.
2 a I was always bored when I went to visit her.
  b She was boring, so I tried not to visit her.
3 a He was excited by the idea for the new invention.
  b His idea for the new invention was exciting.
4 a My mum was very interested in my story.
  b My mum told me a very interesting story.
5 a The walk was very tiring.
  b The walk took a long time because I was tired.
6 a What a fascinating idea!
  b My friend was fascinated by the idea, but I didn't like it.

PLUS

3 Complete the text with the *-ed* or *-ing* form of the adjectives in brackets.

Yoshiro Nakamatsu: A lifetime of invention

Yoshiro Nakamatsu was born in Japan in 1928. His father was a banker and his mother was a teacher, who taught him maths and science. When he was very young, he became (1)__________ (fascinate) with inventing. His parents were (2)__________ (interest) in his inventions. His mother even helped him to register them. Nakamatsu went to university and studied Engineering. He continued to be (3)__________ (excite) about inventing, and has made over 3,000 inventions. Some people say it is closer to 4,000. Some of his inventions are very (4)__________ (surprise), and include a pair of shoes for jumping and a chair that helps you think. Nakamatsu isn't (5)__________ (tire) of inventing yet, even though he is in his 90s. In fact, there are films about him and he sometimes appears on TV shows. He makes people laugh and is not (6)__________ (bore) to watch or listen to. Nakamatsu thinks people can live to be 144 years old and he wants to live to be 144 by taking care of his health.

4 Work with a partner. Compare your answers.

THE PAST CONTINUOUS

GRAMMAR

Forming the past continuous

Use the past continuous to describe actions that were in progress at a specific time in the past.

For positive statements, use *was* / *were* + verb + *-ing*.

He **was studying** Maths last spring.

They **were doing** research for their presentation before class.

For negative statements, use *was* / *were* + *not* + verb + *-ing*.

He **was not / wasn't trying** to invent crisps, but he did.

They **were not / weren't working** at the time.

Use the contractions *wasn't* / *weren't* in everyday speaking. The full forms, *was not* and *were not*, are more common in formal writing.

5 Complete the sentences with the past continuous form of the verbs in brackets.

1 Last year I ____________ (go) to school part-time.
2 John ____________ (work) part-time at a supermarket during the school holidays.
3 In March my sister and I ____________ (live) in Tokyo.
4 We ____________ (not / study) last night. We ____________ (cook) dinner when you called us.
5 At 6 pm yesterday my friends ____________ (travel) to Dubai on a plane.
6 This morning, I ____________ (prepare) a lot of delicious food for a picnic.
7 Last night Fatima ____________ (think) a lot about her family in Oman.
8 Feride ____________ (not / live) in Istanbul last summer.

6 Write four sentences about what you were / weren't doing before class today. Then compare your sentences with a partner. Are any the same?

1 ____________
2 ____________
3 ____________
4 ____________

The past continuous and the past simple

Use the past simple to talk about an action that happened and was completed. Use the past continuous to describe an action which was in progress during a specific time in the past.

He **passed** the exam. (past simple)

He **was studying** for the exam last night. (past continuous)

When / While

Use *when* or *while* with the past simple and past continuous to show when events happened.

main clause — *time clause*

I met Esin **when / while** I was living in Istanbul.

When refers to a particular time when something was in progress or happening.

I met Dr Ramos.
↓
I was living in London. →

main clause — *time clause*

I met Dr Ramos **when** I was living in London.

While means *at* or *during the same time* an event was in progress.

His phone rang.
↓
He was teaching a class. →

main clause — *time clause*

His phone rang **while** he was teaching a class.

Use *when* or *while* and the past continuous to talk about an event that was in progress at the same time a second event happened. Use the past simple for the second event.

event in progress / time clause — *second event / main clause*

While she **was thinking** about the problem, she **had** an idea.

Use *when* (but not *while*) and the past simple to talk about a second event that happened while another event was already in progress. Use the past continuous for the event that was already in progress.

event in progress / main clause — *second event / time clause*

Isaac Newton **was sitting** by a tree when an apple **fell** on his head.

Note: Another way to think of this is that the past simple action 'interrupts' the past continuous action in the example above.

A time clause can come before or after the main clause. Remember to use a comma when the time clause comes first.

Hiro was sleeping **when his phone rang**. **When his phone rang,** Hiro was sleeping.

GRAMMAR

7 Circle the past continuous or the past simple form of the verbs.

In 1895, German scientist Wilhelm Röntgen (1)*experimented* / *was experimenting* with electricity when he (2)*noticed* / *was noticing* something strange about a piece of equipment which created green lights around some objects. While he (3)*watched* / *was watching* the experiment, the rays of the green lights (4)*went* / *were going* through paper, but not thick objects, like bones. On this day, Röntgen (5)*discovered* / *was discovering* X-rays.

In 1945, American engineer Percy Spencer (6)*worked* / *was working* in a lab. One day, while he (7)*did* / *was doing* an experiment, something amazing (8)*happened* / *was happening*. While he (9)*waited* / *was waiting* for the experiment to heat up, he (10)*realized* / *was realizing* that a chocolate bar had melted in his pocket. Spencer (11)*was* / *was being* very surprised. The next day, he (12)*brought* / *was bringing* an egg to the lab. While another scientist (13)*did* / *was doing* the experiment, the egg (14)*blew* / *was blowing* up in his face. On this day, Spencer accidentally (15)*invented* / *was inventing* the microwave oven.

In 1908, a German woman named Melitta Bentz (16)*made* / *was making* an accidental invention. While she (17)*made* / *was making* a cup of coffee, she (18)*discovered* / *was discovering* that paper stopped coffee granules from getting into her cup. On this day, she (19)*created* / *was creating* the coffee filter.

8 Complete the sentences with the past simple or the past continuous form of the words in brackets. Circle *when* or *while*. In some items, more than one answer is possible.

(1)(*When* / *While*) Lina (2)________________ (do) research for her class, she (3)________________ (see) an email from a woman in Japan. The woman had Lina's surname. (4)(*When* / *While*) she (5)________________ (read) the message about the woman's family history, she quickly (6)________________ (realize) that they were cousins.
Last year, Sultan (7)________________ (work) in his office (8)(*when* / *while*) he (9)________________ (drop) his phone. He (10)________________ (look) under his desk for his phone (11)(*when* / *while*) he suddenly (12)________________ (find) 500 euros.

LISTENING 2

PREPARING TO LISTEN

UNDERSTANDING KEY VOCABULARY

1 Read the sentences (1–6). Then write the correct form of the words in bold next to the definitions (a–f).

1 Albert Einstein was a **remarkable** man. He was an extremely intelligent person and did many important things in math and physics.
2 Bette Nesmith Graham had a lot of **success** when she invented correction fluid. Many people wanted to use her invention.
3 Something **amazing** happened in 2013 – in South America, someone discovered a new species. People were shocked because it had been 35 years since the last new animal was found.
4 Sima Najjar is an **entrepreneur**. She created her own business online.
5 Marcus was in a difficult **situation** as a child because both of his parents died.
6 After Jonathan **retired** from being a professor and didn't work anymore, he used his free time to write books.

a ____________ (v) to leave your job and stop working, usually because you get older
b ____________ (adj) very surprising
c ____________ (adj) very unusual or noticeable in a way that you admire
d ____________ (n) the things that are happening and are present at a particular time and place
e ____________ (n) someone who starts his or her own business
f ____________ (n) something that has a good result

PLUS

USING YOUR KNOWLEDGE

2 Work with a partner. You are going to listen to a conversation between students who are preparing for a presentation on interesting people. Discuss the questions.

1 What kind of life do you think an entrepreneur has? Think about his or her job, family and interests. What do you think a typical day would be like?
2 What skills do you need to be an entrepreneur? Do you know any entrepreneurs?

WHILE LISTENING

3 7.2 Listen to the students' conversation about remarkable people. Take notes about who the people are, their jobs and the things they did which were remarkable.

TAKING NOTES ON DETAIL

Person 1

Name:

Job:

Why remarkable:

Person 2

Name:

Job:

Why remarkable:

SKILLS

Listening for attitude

When people speak they don't always say what they think directly. If they don't want to sound negative, they use a positive adjective with a negative verb, e.g. *It isn't very good* instead of *It's bad*. They also weaken a negative statement by using phrases like *a little*. Being aware of this when listening can help you understand what the speaker really means.

4 Answer the questions.

LISTENING FOR ATTITUDE

1 What work do Luisa and Yasmin have to do? ______________________

____

2 Who has done most of their work? ____________________

5 7.2 Listen again. Write words to complete what Luisa says.

1 Actually, I'm ____________________ great.
2 Well ... I haven't done ____________________ .
3 I'm ____________________ at finding things to present.
4 I don't know ____________________ Yoshiro ... .

6 Decide who says the sentences. Write *L* (Luisa) or *Y* (Yasmin).

1 I'm having trouble doing it. __________
2 The introduction's not great. __________
3 It needs a little more work. __________
4 His life doesn't sound that extraordinary. __________
5 Well, I'm not sure I understand everything. __________

7 Write three facts about Sima Najjar and Yoshiro Nakamatsu. Use your notes from Exercise 3 to help you.

Sima Najjar

1 ____

2 ____

3 ____

Yoshiro Nakamatsu

4 ____

5 ____

6 ____

8 Read the *Listening for attitude* explanation box on page 159 again. Which sentences in Exercise 5 ...

a use a positive adjective with a negative verb. _____ _____

b weaken a negative statement by using phrases. _____

9 Luisa does not always say what she thinks directly. Circle the correct word in each sentence that shows what Luisa really thinks.

1 Luisa is feeling *good* / *bad*.
2 Luisa *has prepared* / *hasn't prepared* her presentation.
3 Luisa is *good* / *bad* at finding out things to present.
4 Luisa *knows something* / *doesn't know anything* about Yoshiro Nakamatsu.

PRONUNCIATION FOR LISTENING

SKILLS

Intonation for emotion and interest

When people speak, they show different levels of interest by changing the sound of their voice.

When a speaker is enthusiastic, their voice goes up. Or they may say the word that shows their emotion louder.

That's re↗markable!

When a speaker is unenthusiastic, their voice stays flat or goes down. Or they may say the word that shows their emotion more quietly.

I'm ↗not so ↘good.

10 7.3 Listen to the sentences. Tick the sentences that sound enthusiastic.

1 I'm pretty happy with it. ☐
2 She's a remarkable woman. ☐
3 That's amazing! ☐
4 I'll check him out. ☐

11 Work with a partner. Student A says each of the four sentences either enthusiastically or unenthusiastically. Student B identifies if the intonation is enthusiastic or unenthusiastic. Then change roles.

1 That's good.
2 She's interesting.
3 The weather is fantastic.
4 I'm happy with my work.

DISCUSSION

SYNTHESIZING

12 Work with a partner. Do you think the people in Listening 1 and Listening 2 are remarkable? Why / Why not?

13 Which of the people discussed in Listening 1 and Listening 2 have had the most impact on the world? Give reasons for your answers.

SPEAKING

CRITICAL THINKING

At the end of this unit, you are going to do the speaking task below.

Give a presentation about a remarkable person and his or her work. Describe the impact of this person's work on our lives.

SKILLS

Evaluating the importance of information

Before you use information in a presentation, it is important to evaluate the information. Which information is the most important and should be included? What is less important? Is it interesting? Using an ideas map can help you clearly see what information you have and which ideas are connected or important.

Use an ideas map to think of topics and related subtopics that you want to find information about. Start with your main topic in the centre of the ideas map. Write subtopics on the 'legs' of the ideas map. Use the ideas map to help you do research about your topic and subtopics and to organize the information that you find.

REMEMBER

1 Work with a partner. Fill in the ideas map about Sima Najjar on page 163. Write the letter of each phrase in the bubbles. Use your notes from Exercise 3 in Listening 2 to help you.

- **a** employs young people
- **b** head of modelling company
- **c** 'how to' videos
- **d** worked with female Arab clothing designers
- **e** mother
- **f** viewed by many Saudi Arabian women
- **g** entrepreneur – started online company with videos in Arabic

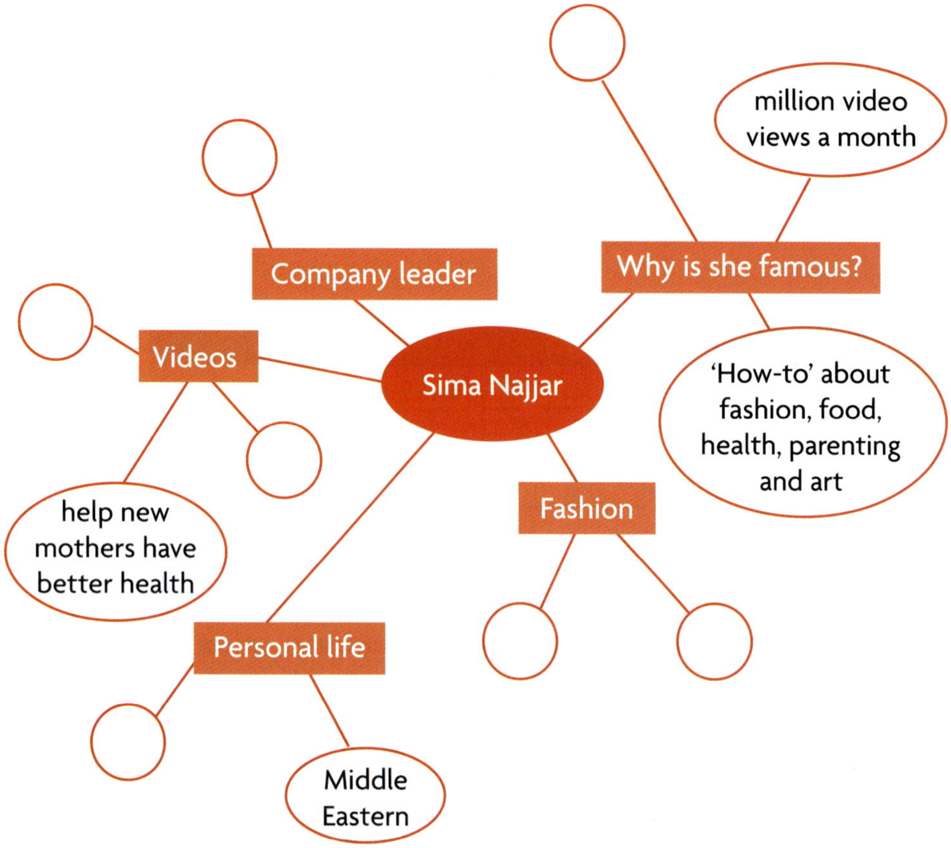

2 Work with a partner. Look at the information in the ideas map in Exercise 1. Which information do you think is most important? If you were going to do the speaking task about Sima Najjar, what information would you include? What would you leave out? Why?

EVALUATE

3 Now think about a remarkable person you would like to find out about. You will do a presentation about this person in the speaking task at the end of this unit.

APPLY

4 Go online and do research about the person. Create an ideas map about the person to organize your ideas.

CREATE

5 Work with a partner. Evaluate your ideas. Which information do you want to include and which do you want to leave out?

PREPARATION FOR SPEAKING

TIME ORDER

SKILLS

When you describe a series of events, for example, the events in someone's life, you can use these words and phrases to show the order in which they happened.

start	middle	end
first (of all) firstly	next then after that	finally

You can also use these words to describe when events happened in relation to one another.

when *nowadays* *at that time* *before* *in* (year)

Nuri Bilge Ceylan is a famous Turkish film director, photographer, writer and actor. **Before** his long career, he took part in cinema and photography clubs at university in Istanbul. **At that time**, he was very interested in photography. He graduated **in** 1985 with a degree in Engineering. **After that**, he went to London, and **then** Kathmandu in Nepal to decide what to do in life. **Next**, he went back to Ankara in Turkey. **When** he was back in Turkey, he realized that cinema was his passion.

Ceylan has won many awards for his work. **First**, he won the Golden Orange award for Best Director **in** 1999. **After that**, he continued to win many other awards for his films. **Finally**, he won his most remarkable award, the Palme d'Or at the Cannes Film Festival **in** 2014. **Nowadays**, Ceylan continues to work on new films and photography that people see around the world.

PLUS

1 Choose the correct time order words and phrases to complete the presentation.

(1)*After that, / Nowadays,* many people know about chocolate chip cookies. But (2)*before / when* 1938, no one had tasted one. (3)*At that time, / Next,* Ruth Graves Wakefield, an American chef, was cooking for the restaurant that she owned with her husband. One day, (4)*in / when* 1938, Wakefield tried to make a chocolate cookie in a new way. (5)*Then / First,* she chopped up a chocolate bar. (6)*Before / Then* she mixed the pieces of chocolate into her cookie dough. (7)*Finally, / When* she baked the cookies, the chocolate didn't melt or mix into the dough like the chocolate she usually used. Instead, the chocolate was just in pieces in the cookies. Wakefield's customers loved the cookies, though. (8)*After that, / When* her chocolate chip cookies became very popular. (9)*Finally, / Firstly,* she made a business deal with the Nestlé company that allowed the company to print her recipe on chocolate chip bags. They sold a lot of chocolate chips over the years, and people still use the same recipe today.

EXAMPLES AND DETAILS

SKILLS

Introducing examples and details to support a presentation

When you give a presentation, it is important to give details and examples. This makes your main ideas easier to understand and more interesting to your audience. You can use these phrases to introduce details and examples:

For example, ...
One example (is / was) ... / Another example (is / was) ...
An important example (is / was) ...
Equally important (is / was) ...
such as ... / also ...

2 7.4 Listen to the student's presentation. Complete the text with the phrases the student uses to introduce examples and details.

My presentation is about Thomas Edison. He was an American inventor and he was born in 1847. He is a remarkable person because he invented a lot of the things we know and use every day, (1)__________________ the electric light bulb. Well, he wasn't the first to invent one, but he *was* the first person to invent one that could last a long time. This was in 1879 while he was working in his research lab in Menlo Park, New Jersey, in the US. It lasted 13.5 hours! (2)__________________ of Edison's amazing inventions is the motion picture camera. We all know this today as the video camera. Edison and his team invented it in 1891 and they showed short six-minute films. (3)__________________ was Edison's work with Henry Ford, who started the Ford Motor Company. Edison was worried about America's dependence on foreign rubber for tyres. So while he was working at a lab in Florida in 1927, he found a new source of rubber in local plants ...

Thomas Edison

3 Work with a partner. Take turns reading the presentation aloud. What other phrases could you use to complete the text?

4 What type of information has the student included about Thomas Edison? Why did they choose this information? Would you have included anything else?

PLUS

SPEAKING TASK

Give a presentation about a remarkable person and his or her work. Describe the impact of this person's work on our lives.

PREPARE

1 Look back at the ideas map you created on page 163 in the Critical thinking section. Add any new information you would like to include.

2 Look at the subtopics in your ideas map. Write sentences you can use in your presentation and put the information in order. Use language from the Preparation for speaking section to help you.

3 Refer to the Task checklist below as you prepare your presentation.

TASK CHECKLIST	✔
Use words and intonation to sound more enthusiastic.	
Use *-ed* and *-ing* adjectives correctly.	
Use time order expressions to show the order in which events took place.	
Use the past continuous and the past simple correctly.	
Give details and examples about the person and his or her work.	

PRESENT

4 Work in small groups. Take turns presenting your person to your group. Take notes on the key points and main information in their presentations while the other members of your group are presenting. When each person has finished presenting, ask questions to find out more about their remarkable person.

5 Decide together as a group which of the people in your presentations is the most remarkable person and why.

OBJECTIVES REVIEW

1 Check your learning objectives for this unit. Write *3*, *2* or *1* for each objective.

3 = very well 2 = well 1 = not so well

I can …

watch and understand a video about art made from rubbish in the sea.	____
listen for attitude.	____
evaluate the importance of information.	____
use the past continuous and the past simple.	____
use time order words and phrases.	____
give examples and details.	____
give a presentation about a remarkable person and his or her work.	____

2 Use the *Unlock* Digital Workbook for more practice with this unit's learning objectives.

UNLOCK ONLINE

WORDLIST

achievement (n) ⊙	fascinating (adj)	simple (adj) ⊙
amazing (adj)	interested (adj) ⊙	situation (n) ⊙
bored (adj)	interesting (adj) ⊙	success (n) ⊙
boring (adj)	invention (n) ⊙	surprised (adj)
complicated (adj) ⊙	point (n) ⊙	surprising (adj) ⊙
design (n) ⊙	purpose (n) ⊙	tired (adj)
entrepreneur (n)	relaxed (adj)	tiring (adj)
excited (adj) ⊙	relaxing (adj)	use (n) ⊙
exciting (adj) ⊙	remarkable (adj) ⊙	
fascinated (adj)	retire (v)	

⊙ = high-frequency words in the Cambridge Academic Corpus

LEARNING OBJECTIVES	IN THIS UNIT YOU WILL ...
Watch and listen	watch and understand a video about the Voyager space project.
Listening skill	understand meaning from context.
Critical thinking	find the best solution to a problem.
Grammar	use the second conditional.
Speaking skills	take turns in a discussion; show levels of agreement.
Speaking task	discuss how to get children interested in space exploration.

THE UNIVERSE

UNIT 8

UNLOCK YOUR KNOWLEDGE

Work with a partner. Look at the photo and answer the questions.

1 What is the machine in the photo? What does it do?
2 What types of things can we learn from studying the night sky?
3 Huge amounts of money are spent on studying space and space exploration. Do you think we should spend so much money on this research? Why / Why not?

PLUS

WATCH AND LISTEN

PREPARING TO WATCH

ACTIVATING YOUR KNOWLEDGE

1 Work with a partner. Answer the questions.

1 What are the names of the eight planets in our solar system?
2 What else is there in space?
3 Do you think learning about space is important? Why / Why not?

PREDICTING CONTENT USING VISUALS

2 You are going to watch a video about the Voyager space project. Look at the photos from the video. What are the people doing?

GLOSSARY

NASA (n) the National Aeronautics and Space Administration, the US government organization that plans and controls American space travel and studies space
dish (n) a round piece of equipment that receives information from objects in space
speed of light (n) how fast light moves (about 300 million metres per second)
solar system (n) the sun and the planets, such as Earth and Saturn, that move around it

WHILE WATCHING

UNDERSTANDING DETAIL

3 Watch the video. Complete the sentences with a number or word from the box. Then compare your answers with a partner.

11	17	1977	2012	space	years

1 Voyager began its journey in ______ .
2 Almost 40 ______ later, Voyager still communicates with a dish.
3 It communicates with this dish over ______ billion miles away.
4 Voyager's message takes more than ______ hours to get to Earth.
5 The little green triangle shows Voyager in deep ______ .
6 In ______ , Voyager left our solar system.

4 Read the questions and circle the correct answer.

1 Where does NASA communicate with Voyager from?
 a The Mojave Desert in California   b Kennedy Space Station in Texas
2 Who is the scientist for the Voyager project?
 a Dr Edmund Halley   b Dr Edward Stone
3 What planets did Voyager fly by?
 a Mars, Venus, Jupiter and Mercury   b Jupiter, Saturn, Uranus and Neptune
4 How fast does a message travel from Voyager to the dish?
 a at the speed of light   b at the speed of sound
5 Where did Voyager 1 become the first man-made object to ever travel to?
 a outside the solar system   b inside the solar system

5 Watch again and check your answers to Exercise 4.

UNDERSTANDING MAIN IDEAS

6 Answer the questions.

1 What was Voyager's goal when it flew by the planets?
2 Did the Voyager team know how long Voyager could survive?
3 What is NASA learning from Voyager?

DISCUSSION

7 Work in small groups. Discuss the questions.

1 What are some things we learn from space organizations like NASA?
2 Do you think working for NASA would be exciting? Why / Why not?
3 Why might it be difficult to work for NASA?

8 Look at the ways to send messages in the box. Then answer the questions.

by phone	by post	by text	by email

1 What is the fastest way to send a message? What's the slowest way?
2 How do you know when someone gets your message?
3 Can messages be saved or deleted for each way? How?
4 Which way do you prefer to send messages? Why?

LISTENING

LISTENING 1

PRONUNCIATION FOR LISTENING

WORDS WITH EASILY-CONFUSED SOUNDS

1 8.1 Listen to the sentences. Underline two words in each sentence which sound the same.

1 When the sun is out, I make sure my son uses sunscreen so he doesn't get sunburnt.
2 Have you read the information about the Red Planet?
3 We are having a picnic, whether it is hot or not. It has been good weather recently, so we are hoping it will be nice.
4 She ate her dinner before she went out at eight o'clock.
5 There are two doctors in the family, and their daughter is also studying medicine.
6 Our guest was in the house for an hour.

2 Work with a partner. Take turns saying the pairs of words aloud. What do you notice about the spelling and the sound of the words?

1	weather /weðə/	whether /weðə/
2	our /aʊə/	hour /aʊə/
3	sun /sʌn/	son /sʌn/
4	read /red/	red /red/
5	there /ðeə/	their /ðeə/
6	sent /sent/	scent /sent/
7	ate /eɪt/	eight /eɪt/
8	mined /maɪnd/	mind /maɪnd/
9	for /fɔː/	four /fɔː/
10	too /tuː/	two /tuː/

3 8.2 Listen and write the sentences.

1 ____________________
2 ____________________
3 ____________________
4 ____________________
5 ____________________
6 ____________________

PREPARING TO LISTEN

UNDERSTANDING KEY VOCABULARY

4 You are going to listen to a radio programme about space travel. Read the definitions. Then complete the sentences with the correct form of the words in bold.

> **beyond** (prep) on the other side of something
> **explore** (v) to travel around a place to find out what is there
> **journey** (n) a long trip from one place to another
> **path** (n) the direction that a person or thing moves in
> **planet** (n) a large, round object in space that moves around the sun or another star
> **reach** (v) to arrive somewhere
> **spacecraft** (n) a vehicle that can travel into space
> **surface** (n) the top or outside part of something

1 Scientists are trying to develop a __________ that can carry people all the way to Mars.
2 In our solar system, Earth is the only __________ humans can live on. Some people think that Mars could be a home for humans one day.
3 Researchers want to go deep into space and __________ other solar systems. There is a lot we could learn from research in space.
4 It takes about three days for a spacecraft to travel the 386,400 kilometres from Earth to the moon. That's a long __________ .
5 Earth's __________ is made up of large masses of land and large bodies of water.
6 Scientists hope to __________ Mars by the year 2030. Right now, only robots and satellites have arrived there.
7 The moon follows a __________ around Earth. Similarly, Earth follows one around the sun.
8 Scientists sent a satellite __________ our own solar system. We now have more information about places farther away from Earth.

WHILE LISTENING

SKILLS

Understanding meaning from context

Some words sound the same or very similar. If the words sound the same, you have to guess from the context which word is correct. Also, think about which type of word it is. For example, *read* is a verb, but *red* is an adjective.

5 8.3 Listen to the first part of the radio programme. Complete the sentences with the words you hear.

1 We'll think about the planets people haven't visited yet and __________ we are likely to visit some of them in the future.
2 Let's begin inside our own solar system, which is made up of all the planets and the __________ .
3 Mars is known as the '__________ Planet' because of its colour.
4 NASA, the US government organization that studies space, so far has only __________ robot explorers to Mars.
5 Even with the danger, many people want __________ travel to Mars.

6 Read the sentences in Exercise 5 again and check the spelling of the words you wrote.

TAKING NOTES ON DETAIL

7 8.4 Listen to the second part of the radio programme. Complete the student's outline.

1 NASA plans to send people to asteroid
- A Send to asteroid by (1)__________ ; asteroid = very large rock goes around (2)__________
  - 1 Robot reaches asteroid and takes a large (3)__________
  - 2 Robot sends it on a path around (4)__________
  - 3 People (5)__________ asteroid piece in 2020s; travel on Orion spacecraft
- B Other uses for Orion
  - 1 No travel to Mars
  - 2 (6)__________ new spacecraft

2 Lucy – BPM 37093
- A (7)__________ star = white dwarf star
  - 1 Doesn't burn, shines with (8)__________
  - 2 Huge diamond
  - 3 It is (9)__________ our solar system
- B Facts about Lucy
  - 1 About (10)__________ kilometres across
  - 2 Smaller than Earth – half as wide
  - 3 Hot, with temperature of about 2,700 °C
  - 4 Only half as (11)__________ as our sun

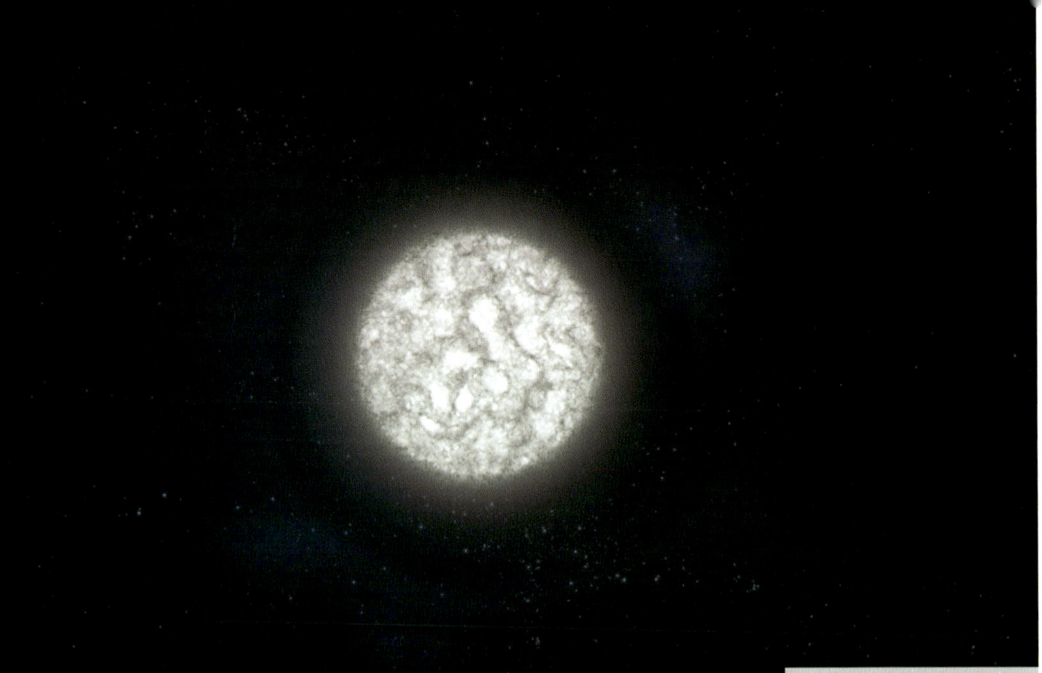

a white dwarf star

8 Write *T* (true) or *F* (false) next to the statements below. Then correct the false statements.

_____ 1 NASA plans to have robots take a boulder from an asteroid and send it around the moon.

____

_____ 2 White dwarf stars are found in our solar system.

____

_____ 3 Lucy is larger than Earth.

____

_____ 4 Lucy is bigger than all of the diamonds found on Earth.

____

_____ 5 A human trip to Mars is planned for the 2020s.

____

9 8.4 Listen to the second part of the programme again. Write down one more piece of information about NASA's plans for Mars exploration and one more piece of information about the dwarf star Lucy.

1 ______________________________
2 ______________________________

DISCUSSION

10 Work with a partner. Discuss the questions.

1 What are some possible reasons why people want to go to Mars?
2 What would be some of the benefits of being able to go there?
3 What do you think about a robot bringing an asteroid boulder to orbit the moon? What could be dangerous about that?

LANGUAGE DEVELOPMENT

VOCABULARY FOR PROBLEMS AND SOLUTIONS

1 Read the sentences. Then complete the table with the words in bold.

1. We will talk about the **issue** of paying for space exploration.
2. What is the **impact** of space exploration on people today? Does it make our lives better?
3. What **options** do we have for paying for things like going to Mars? Is there more than one way to pay?
4. One **alternative** to the government paying for space research is private companies doing it.
5. If we don't have enough money for space exploration, it is a **problem** because then scientists cannot continue the very important research they are doing.
6. It seems that a **solution** to the problem of not having enough money could be to tax the companies that make a profit from space exploration.
7. When people stay in space for a long time, what **effects** are there? Do they get sick more or do they have trouble when they come back to Earth?

A word	B definition
a option	(n) a choice
b effect	(n) a change, reaction or result that is caused by something
c ________	(n) the answer to the problem
d ________	(n) the effect that a person, event or situation has on someone or something
e ________	(n) a situation that causes difficulties and needs to be solved
f ________	(n) an important topic or problem that people are discussing
g ________	(n) one of two or more things you can choose between

2 Which words in the table have similar meanings?

3 Complete the sentences with the words from Exercise 1. In some items, more than one answer is possible.

1 One __________ with going to Mars is that we don't have enough information about how to survive once we get there.
2 What is the __________ that we will discuss in class on Friday? I want to read more about it before then, so that I have enough support for my ideas.
3 In the future, will there be a(n) __________ to travel to space as a tourist or will only scientists be able to go?
4 What type of __________ would there be if we stopped exploring space? What do you think would happen?
5 There are about 500,000 pieces of space junk (old broken things in space) orbiting Earth that could harm a spacecraft. But the only __________ for a spacecraft to not get hit is to try to move out of the way of the junk.
6 I don't see any __________ to having governments pay for at least part of space research. Companies only want to pay for things that will make money, not for things that are just interesting to know.
7 What __________ does the moon have on people? Does a full moon cause things to happen on our planet or affect things in nature?

PLUS

THE SECOND CONDITIONAL

GRAMMAR

Use the second conditional to describe imagined situations that would happen under certain conditions in the present or future.

Use the past simple in the *if*-clause to describe the imagined situation. Use a modal verb (e.g. *would / could*) in the main clause to describe the predicted result or possible outcome.

The *if*-clause can come before or after the main clause. Use a comma between the clauses when the *if*-clause comes first.

if-clause | *main clause*

If we **had** the right spacecraft, we **would send** people to Mars.

main clause | *if-clause*

We **would send** people to Mars if we **had** the right spacecraft.

Notice that in the *if*-clause, the past form *were* (*be*) is used for all persons (*I, you, we, they, he, she, it*).

If a very light spacesuit **were** invented, people could walk around on Mars easily.

4 Complete the second conditional sentences with the words in brackets. Use *would* or *could* in the main clause.

1 If I became (become) an astronaut, I could go (go) to the moon.
2 If I ________ (meet) the president, I ________________ (not / know) what to say.
3 I ________ (become) an astronaut if I ________ (study) Astrophysics.
4 If I ________ (be) more patient, I ________ (get) a PhD in Physics.
5 If I ________ (not / be) busy next week, I ________ (go) to the meeting.
6 Robyn ________________ (think) of good solutions if she ________ (understand) the issue.
7 The programme ________ (be) more likely to succeed if the government ________ (give) more money.
8 If more interesting things ________ (happen), more people ________ (be) willing to give money to the project.

PLUS

5 Complete the predictions about the future with your own ideas (1–4). Then write two of your own predictions (5 and 6).

1 If NASA sent people to Mars in the 2030s, ________________________________.
2 If more people studied Astrophysics and Astronomy, ________________________________.
3 If space travel were as easy as travelling on a plane, ________________________________.
4 If the government stopped paying for space exploration, ________________________________.
5 ________________________________.
6 ________________________________.

6 Work with a partner. Compare your sentences from Exercise 5. Are your predictions similar or different? Which do you think are more likely to happen?

LISTENING 2

PREPARING TO LISTEN

UNDERSTANDING KEY VOCABULARY

1 You are going to listen to a discussion about the ways to pay for space exploration. Read the sentences (1–6). Then choose the best definition (a or b) for the words in bold.

1 We have two **options** for exploring Mars – we can send robots or we can send people.
   a choices
   b opinions
2 The American space organization NASA has a **public** part of their website where anyone in the world can see their projects and offer ideas for how to use some of their inventions.
   a only for one person or group and not for everyone
   b open to everyone to see or use
3 **Private** companies want to do research into space exploration. They do not receive money from the government and they pay for the research themselves.
   a controlled by a person or a company and not by the government
   b controlled by the government and not by a person or company
4 An astronomer is an **expert** in the study of space. He or she often has a PhD degree in the field.
   a someone who does not have enough knowledge about something
   b someone who has a lot of knowledge about something
5 The company hired a recent university graduate who had a lot of **talent**. The company was very happy that its new employee could do the job so well.
   a a natural ability to do something
   b good grades, e.g. in your university exams
6 The supervisor **evaluated** the project to see if it was good enough for the company to continue to spend money on it.
   a fixed something so that it was of the appropriate standard
   b considered or studied something carefully to decide how good or bad it was

PLUS

PREDICTING CONTENT USING VISUALS

2 Work with a partner. Look at the photo and answer the questions.

1 Do photos like these make you feel interested in learning more about space exploration? Why / Why not?
2 Who do you think pays for exploring space?

NASA's *Curiosity* Mars rover

WHILE LISTENING

LISTENING FOR MAIN IDEAS

3 8.5 Listen to the first part of the talk introducing the discussion. Complete the sentences.

1 We'll begin today's discussion with a look at how to pay for space __________ .
2 We'll also evaluate the __________ of space exploration and whether the money we spend is worth it. We will first look at the __________ for paying for space exploration.

4 You are going to listen to the second part of the discussion. What do you think the purpose of the discussion will be? Choose the most likely option.

1 to describe what space exploration is like
2 to think about options for paying for space exploration and the good and bad points of exploring space
3 to make a new plan for future space exploration and for humans living on other planets

5 Work with a partner. Compare your predictions from Exercise 4. Do you agree?

possible future settlement on Mars

6 Work with a partner. Predict the topics that you think will be included in the second part of the discussion.

1 time taken to travel to other parts of space
2 the benefits of space exploration
3 current space exploration projects
4 money spent on space exploration
5 the number of people working in space exploration
6 who pays for space explorers

7 8.6 Listen to the second part of the discussion. Complete the student's notes.

TAKING NOTES ON DETAIL

speaker	opinion	reason
Dr Jun Wu	Wants funding from (1) ________	Space exploration is (2) ________ Space explorations shows us how (3) ________, what stars do, the effects on people in space
Raj Padow	Wants funding from (4) ________	Because companies get (5) ________ from discoveries made in space exploration
Dorota Loy	Wants (6) ________ money for exploration	Because (7) ________ benefits from space exploration Get funding from governments, private companies and private (8) ________ People around the world giving money on (9) ________

8 8.6 Listen again. Use your notes to check your answers to Exercises 4 and 6.

DISCUSSION

SYNTHESIZING

9 Work in small groups. Use ideas from Listening 1 and Listening 2 to discuss the following questions.

1 Do you think people should try to go to Mars? Why / Why not?
2 Who do you think should pay for space exploration? Why? Have you changed your mind based on what you have learnt in this unit?

10 Work with a partner. Look at the pictures below and on pages 180 and 181 and discuss the questions. Use your notes to support your answers.

1 Do you think people will live on Mars in the future? If yes, in what year?
2 What would be the advantages or disadvantages for people?
3 Would you like to visit or live there? Why / Why not? If you lived there, what would you do in your free time?

PLUS

SPEAKING

CRITICAL THINKING

At the end of this unit, you are going to do the speaking task below.

Discuss how to get children interested in space exploration.

SKILLS

Finding the best solution to a problem

When you are trying to work out a solution to a problem, you are unlikely to find the best answer right away. A good strategy is to think of several solutions. Then evaluate them, to decide which is the best.

REMEMBER

1 Work with a partner. Look back at your notes from Listening 2. What is the main problem that the speakers discuss? Write your answer in the *problem* column of the table.

<table>
<tr><td rowspan="4">problem</td><td>possible solution 1</td></tr>
<tr><td>possible solution 2</td></tr>
<tr><td>possible solution 3</td></tr>
<tr><td>possible solution 4</td></tr>
</table>

2 What solutions did the speakers suggest? Write your answers in the *possible solution* sections in the table.

EVALUATE

3 Which of the four possible solutions do you think is best? Why? Compare your answer with a partner.

APPLY

4 Look at the speaking task on page 183. What problems do you think you might face in getting children interested in space exploration? Add them to the ideas map below.

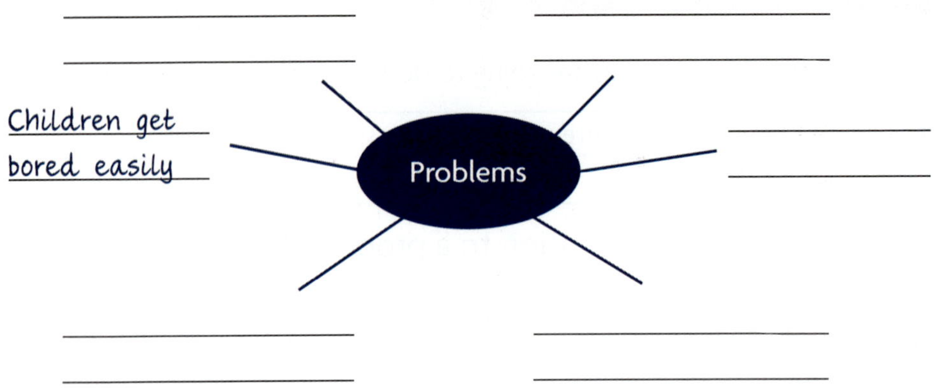

EVALUATE

5 Compare your problems from Exercise 4 with a partner. Which of the problems do you think is the most serious? Why?

ANALYZE

6 Choose one of the problems you identified in Exercise 4, or one from the list below (1–4). Then complete the table with the problem and possible solutions. You will use this information in the speaking task at the end of this unit.

1 We are in a city and in cities it is hard to see the stars.
2 Children these days want fast-moving entertainment, like video games and television, so they might get bored.
3 Equipment like telescopes can be expensive and we don't have much money.
4 Our astronomy club is in a small town far away from astronomy experts, such as university professors. How can we find an expert to help us?

problem	possible solution 1
	possible solution 2
	possible solution 3
	possible solution 4

7 Work in small groups. Take turns sharing your solutions to the problem you chose. Does your group agree with your possible solutions?

8 Work in the same group. Discuss the questions about problem solving.

ANALYZE

1 Can you think of any other ways to organize your ideas about problems and solutions? Look back at the different tables in the units of the book to help you.
2 What kind of information can you give to support your ideas for possible solutions? Think of supporting ideas you can add to the table in Exercise 6 to help you.

PREPARATION FOR SPEAKING

TURN-TAKING

1 People often use fixed phrases to invite others to speak, interrupt or continue speaking when someone has stopped them. Complete the table with the turn-taking phrases.

a What is your opinion?
b Could I finish?
c I'd like to finish my point.
d Could I just say something?
e Sorry, but I have to interrupt you and say ...
f You haven't said much. What do you think?
g Why don't you start us off ... ?
h Sorry, but can I just say ... ?
i Would anybody like to say anything else about ... ?
j Let me just finish what I was saying.

inviting someone else to speak	interrupting	continuing to speak
Let's get your thoughts on this.	Could I just say something here?	Could I finish my point? Please allow me to finish.

2 Complete the dialogue with phrases from Exercise 1. In some items, more than one answer is possible.

Halil: We are discussing the best way to travel. (1)__________________, Ramona?

Ramona: For me, it is definitely by train. You can relax and watch the world go by as you travel and ...

Shin: (2)__________________? Doesn't that depend on the train? In many cities, you can't sit down. Trains are too crowded and ...

Ramona: (3)__________________. You can relax and watch the world go by, but that's in a city where the trains are not too busy.

Halil: (4)______________________________ trains?

Lisa: No, but I'd like to talk about bikes. They are the cheapest way to travel.

Ramona: I agree. It is another good way to travel.

Halil: And Roberto, (5)__________________? (6)__________________?

Roberto: Sorry! I wasn't listening!

3 Work in small groups. Read the dialogue aloud.

4 Divide the phrases into those we use to start a discussion and those we use to finish a discussion. Write *S* (start) or *F* (finish).

1 Let me begin by asking ... ______
2 Let me end this by saying ... ______
3 We'll begin today's discussion by ... ______
4 Would you like to start? ______
5 So, to conclude ... ______
6 Finally, ... ______

SHOWING LEVELS OF AGREEMENT

SKILLS

In discussions it is important to let others know that you understand their points and how much you agree with them. You can show you agree with someone by using these phrases:

Phrases showing strong agreement:

I agree with you completely / 100 percent.
You're absolutely right.
I feel exactly the same.
That's a good point.

You can let others know that you have understood their points, even if you don't agree with them, by using these phrases:

Phrases showing weak agreement or understanding (but maybe not agreeing):

I suppose / guess so.
You could / might be right.
You have a point.
I see your point.
I hear what you're saying, (but) ...

5 Complete the dialogue with phrases from the box. Use the words in brackets to help you choose phrases for strong or weak agreement. In some items, more than one answer is possible.

Ela: I think that it is really important for children to have an interest in space exploration – we need to make sure these important programmes continue into the future.

Carlos: (1)____________________ . (weak) But do you think we really need a lot of kids interested in space?

Hao: Hmm. Carlos, (2)____________________ , (weak) but Ela has a good point. Even if people don't work on space exploration, we still need engineers so we have satellites in orbit for our phones and GPS.

Ela: (3)____________________ , (strong) Hao. And we have satellites for predicting the weather, too.

Carlos: (4)____________________ . (strong) I don't want to lose those things. But I don't think kids need to get interested in living on Mars.

Ela: Hmm. (5)____________________ . (weak) Well, who knows what will happen with global warming and our future. Don't you think it would be good to have some options?

Hao: I think both of (6)____________________ . (weak) Still, maybe it is good to at least ensure children know about space exploration.

PLUS

SPEAKING TASK

Discuss how to get children interested in space exploration.

PREPARE

1 Look back at your notes on page 184 in the Critical thinking section. Add any new information to the table.

2 Work in small groups. Share your ideas for how you can get children interested in space exploration. Follow these steps:

- Use the table in Exercise 6 in the Critical thinking section to help you.
- Make sure that you discuss possible problems and solutions.
- Use the language from the Preparation for speaking section to take turns in your discussion, to show different levels of agreement and to acknowledge other people's ideas.

3 You are going to discuss your ideas with another group. Choose which points from your discussion in Exercise 2 you will discuss.

4 Refer to the Task checklist below as you prepare for your discussion.

TASK CHECKLIST	✔
Use phrases to acknowledge and agree with others' points.	
Use vocabulary for problems and solutions.	
Use the second conditional correctly.	
Use phrases for turn-taking.	

DISCUSS

5 Work with another group. Take turns discussing your ideas. Take notes on other people's ideas and any problems you see with their plans. Ask follow-up questions.

6 In the same group, decide which ideas are best.

7 Compare your final plan with other groups. Which is the best plan?

OBJECTIVES REVIEW

1 Check your learning objectives for this unit. Write *3*, *2* or *1* for each objective.

3 = very well 2 = well 1 = not so well

I can …

watch and understand a video about the Voyager space project.	_____
understand meaning from context.	_____
find the best solution to a problem.	_____
use the second conditional.	_____
take turns in a discussion.	_____
show levels of agreement.	_____
discuss how to get children interested in space exploration.	_____

2 Use the *Unlock* Digital Workbook for more practice with this unit's learning objectives.

UNLOCK ONLINE

WORDLIST

alternative (n) ⊙	issue (n) ⊙	public (adj) ⊙
beyond (prep) ⊙	journey (n) ⊙	reach (v) ⊙
effect (n) ⊙	option (n) ⊙	solution (n) ⊙
evaluate (v) ⊙	path (n) ⊙	spacecraft (n)
expert (n) ⊙	planet (n) ⊙	surface (n)
explore (v) ⊙	private (adj) ⊙	talent (n) ⊙
impact (n) ⊙	problem (n) ⊙	

⊙ = high-frequency words in the Cambridge Academic Corpus

PAIRWORK EXERCISES

UNIT 5

Exercise 4, page 117

ROLE CARD STUDENT A

You are the parent of someone who wants to become a professional athlete. What do you think about the money spent on athletes? Why? After you have completed the persuasion map on page 118, you can use it to help you.

ROLE CARD STUDENT B

You are a charity worker. Your charity helps poor people get food and medicine. What do you think about the money spent on athletes? Why? After you have completed the persuasion map on page 118, you can use it to help you.

ROLE CARD STUDENT C

You are a journalist and you write about sports for a newspaper. What do you think about the money spent on athletes? Why? After you have completed the persuasion map on page 118, you can use it to help you.

ROLE CARD STUDENT D

You are a famous footballer. What do you think about the money spent on athletes? Why? After you have completed the persuasion map on page 118, you can use it to help you.

UNIT 6

Exercise 4, page 143

STUDENT A

1 Tell student B your problems at work. Use the ideas below. Then listen to student B's advice.

   1 Everyone is late for meetings and wastes my time.
   2 When I have to speak English in a meeting, I get too nervous to speak.
   3 I can't use the computer very well.

2 Listen to student B's problems. Give him or her some advice.

STUDENT B

1 Listen to student A's problems. Give him or her some advice.

2 Tell student A your problems at work. Use the ideas below. Then listen to student A's advice.

   1 People leave the meeting room very messy after meetings and I have to clean it up.
   2 I keep forgetting meetings and appointments.
   3 I find it difficult to do presentations because I get too nervous.

GLOSSARY

⊙ = high-frequency words in the Cambridge Academic Corpus

Vocabulary	Pronunciation	Part of speech	Definition
UNIT 1			
ancient ⊙	/'eɪnʃənt/	(adj)	from a long time ago; very old
apartment	/ə'pɑːtmənt/	(n)	a room or set of rooms in a building for someone to live in
area ⊙	/'eəriə/	(n)	a part of a larger place
be located ⊙	/biː ləʊ'keɪtɪd/	(v)	to be in a particular place
bridge ⊙	/brɪdʒ/	(n)	something built over a river or road that lets people, cars or trains go across
capital ⊙	/'kæpɪtəl/	(n)	the most important city in a country or state, where the government is
cave	/keɪv/	(n)	a large hole in the side of a mountain or under the ground
cheap ⊙	/tʃiːp/	(adj)	not expensive, or costing less than usual
crowded	/'kraʊdɪd/	(adj)	very full of people
expensive ⊙	/ɪk'spensɪv/	(adj)	costing a lot of money
field ⊙	/fiːld/	(n)	open, grassy land
lake ⊙	/leɪk/	(n)	a body of water that has land all around it
modern ⊙	/'mɒdən/	(adj)	relating to the present time and not to the past
popular ⊙	/'pɒpjələ/	(adj)	liked by many people
recognize ⊙	/'rekəgnaɪz/	(v)	to know something because you have seen it before
rock ⊙	/rɒk/	(n)	a hard piece of the material that the Earth is made of
rural ⊙	/'rʊərəl/	(adj)	relating to the countryside and not to cities or towns
strange ⊙	/streɪndʒ/	(adj)	different from the usual or normal; unusual or not expected
traffic ⊙	/'træfɪk/	(n)	all the cars and trucks using the road

Vocabulary	Pronunciation	Part of speech	Definition
urban	/ˈɜːbən/	(adj)	belonging to or related to a city
woods	/wʊdz/	(n)	a place with a lot of trees growing near each other

UNIT 2

Vocabulary	Pronunciation	Part of speech	Definition
activity	/ækˈtɪvəti/	(n)	something you do for enjoyment, especially an organized event
celebrate	/ˈseləbreɪt/	(v)	to do something fun because it is a special day or because something good has happened
costume	/ˈkɒstjuːm/	(n)	clothes that people wear to make them look like someone or something else
culture	/ˈkʌltʃə/	(n)	the habits and traditions of a country or group of people
decorate	/ˈdekəreɪt/	(v)	to make something look pretty by putting things on it
dish	/dɪʃ/	(n)	one type of food prepared as part of a bigger meal
enjoy	/ɪnˈdʒɔɪ/	(v)	get pleasure from
entertainment	/ˌentəˈteɪnmənt/	(n)	shows, films, games or other ways of having fun
firework	/ˈfaɪəwɜːk/	(n)	a small object which explodes to make a loud noise and bright colours, and is often used for special events
gift	/gɪft/	(n)	something special that you give to someone else
have a celebration / have a party	/hæv ə seləˈbreɪʃən/ /hæv ə ˈpɑːti/	(phr)	to have a social event where a group of people meet to talk, eat, etc., often in order to celebrate a special occasion
have fun / have a nice time	/hæv ˈfʌn/ /hæv ə ˈnaɪs taɪm/	(phr)	to enjoy yourself
have a problem	/hæv ə ˈprɒbləm/	(phr)	to be in a situation that needs to be dealt with or solved
lecture	/ˈlektʃə/	(n)	a formal talk about a subject

Vocabulary	Pronunciation	Part of speech	Definition
parade	/pə'reɪd/	(n)	a line of people or vehicles that moves through the streets to celebrate a special day or event
take care (of)	/teɪk 'keər/	(phr v)	to be careful (to be in charge of someone or something)
take part	/teɪk 'pɑːt/	(phr v)	to be involved in an activity with other people
take place	/teɪk 'pleɪs/	(phr v)	to happen
traditional	/trə'dɪʃənəl/	(adj)	part of older ways of doing things and older ideas that are not modern
UNIT 3			
accident	/'æksɪdənt/	(n)	something bad that happens, that is not on purpose and which causes injury or damage
app	/æp/	(n)	a computer program with a particular purpose
battery	/'bætəri/	(n)	an object that provides electricity for things such as radios, toys, or cars
charge	/tʃɑːdʒ/	(v)	to put electricity into something
charger	/'tʃɑːdʒə/	(n)	a piece of equipment used for putting electricity in a battery
collect	/kə'lekt/	(v)	to get things from different places and bring them together
develop	/dɪ'veləp/	(v)	to make something new
disabled	/dɪ'seɪbld/	(adj)	having an illness or injury that makes it difficult to do the things that other people can do
file	/faɪl/	(n)	a collection of information stored in one place on a computer
go online	/gəʊ ɒn'laɪn/	(phr)	to spend time connected to the internet
information	/ˌɪnfə'meɪʃən/	(n)	facts about a situation, person, event, etc.
key	/kiː/	(n)	one of the parts you press on a computer keyboard to produce letters and numbers

Vocabulary	Pronunciation	Part of speech	Definition
keyboard	/'kiːbɔːd/	(n)	a set of keys on a computer that you press to make it work
laptop	/'læptɒp/	(n)	a small computer that you can carry around with you
location	/ləʊ'keɪʃən/	(n)	a place where something is found
log in	/lɒg ɪn/	(v)	to connect a computer to a system of computers by typing your name and a password
luxury	/'lʌkʃəri/	(n)	something expensive that you enjoy but do not need
memory	/'meməri/	(n)	the ability to remember
mouse	/maʊs/	(n)	a thing that you move with your hand to control what a computer does
PC	/ˌpiː'siː/	(n)	A personal computer (= a computer for one person to use)
research	/rɪ'sɜːtʃ/	(n)	a detailed study of a subject to learn more about it
robot	/'rəʊbɒt/	(n)	a machine which can do things that people can do
shut down	/ʃʌt 'daʊn/	(v)	if a computer shuts down or someone shuts it down, it stops operating
stupid	/'stjuːpɪd/	(adj)	silly or not intelligent
suit	/suːt/	(n)	an outfit of a jacket and trousers or a jacket and skirt made of the same material
surf the internet	/sɜːf ðə 'ɪntənet/	(phr)	to look at information on the internet by moving from one page to another
text	/tekst/	(n)	a message sent from a mobile phone
text	/tekst/	(v)	to send a message from a mobile phone
the cloud	/ðə 'klaʊd/	(n)	a computer network where files and programs can be stored, especially the internet

Vocabulary	Pronunciation	Part of speech	Definition
turn off	/tɜːn 'ɒf/	(v)	to move the switch on a machine, light, etc. so that it stops working, or to stop the supply of water, electricity, etc.
turn on	/tɜːn 'ɒn/	(v)	to move the switch on a machine, light, etc. so that it starts working, or to start the supply of water, electricity, etc.
Wi-Fi	/'waɪfaɪ/	(n)	a system used for connecting computers and other electronic equipment to the internet without using wires
UNIT 4			
angry	/'æŋgri/	(adj)	having a strong feeling that makes you want to shout at someone or hurt them
become	/bɪ'kʌm/	(v)	to begin to be something
believe	/bɪ'liːv/	(v)	to think that something is true and correct
carefully	/'keəfəl.i/	(adv)	with great attention
cool	/kuːl/	(adj)	slightly cold; of a low temperature
cut down	/kʌt 'daʊn/	(v)	to make a tree or other plant fall to the ground by cutting it near the bottom
disappear	/ˌdɪsə'pɪə/	(v)	to stop existing in the world
discover	/dɪ'skʌvə/	(v)	to find something for the first time
dry	/draɪ/	(adj)	without water or liquid
energy	/'enədʒi/	(n)	the power and ability to do something or be active
forest fire	/'fɒrɪst faɪə/	(n)	a fire burning in an area of land with many trees, that is difficult to control and sometimes spreads quickly
global warming	/gləʊbəl 'wɔːmɪŋ/	(n)	an increase in the temperature of the air around the world because of pollution
humid	/'hjuːmɪd/	(adj)	having a lot of moisture in the air

Vocabulary	Pronunciation	Part of speech	Definition
look after	/lʊk 'ɑːftə/	(v)	to take care of someone or something by keeping them healthy or in a good condition
prefer	/prɪ'fɜː/	(v)	to choose or want one thing instead of another
prevent	/prɪ'vent/	(v)	to stop something happening or to stop someone doing something
rainforest	/'reɪnˌfɒrɪst/	(n)	a forest with a lot of tall trees where it rains a lot
save	/seɪv/	(v)	to bring something back to good condition; to keep something from harm
unusual	/ʌn'juːʒuəl/	(adj)	different from what is common or expected
upset	/ʌp'set/	(adj)	unhappy or worried because something unpleasant has happened
wildlife	/'waɪldlaɪf/	(n)	animals, birds and plants living in their natural environment

UNIT 5

Vocabulary	Pronunciation	Part of speech	Definition
champion	/'tʃæmpiən/	(n)	someone who wins a competition
charge	/tʃɑːdʒ/	(v)	to ask someone to pay for something, especially for an activity or a service
compete	/kəm'piːt/	(v)	to do an activity with others and try to do it better than they do
competition	/ˌkɒmpə'tɪʃən/	(n)	an organized event in which people try to win by being the best, the fastest, etc.
cost	/kɒst/	(n)	the amount of money that you need to buy or do something
fan	/fæn/	(n)	someone who likes a famous person, sport, type of music, etc.
hit	/hɪt/	(v)	to touch something quickly and forcefully with the hand or an object
intelligent	/ɪn'telɪdʒənt/	(adj)	able to understand and learn well
kick	/kɪk/	(v)	to hit someone or something with the foot

Vocabulary	Pronunciation	Part of speech	Definition
prize	/praɪz/	(n)	something valuable that is given to someone who wins a game or has done good work
salary	/'sæləri/	(n)	the amount of money that you get from your job, usually paid every month
score	/skɔː/	(v)	to get points in a game or in a test
strong	/strɒŋ/	(adj)	physically powerful
support	/sə'pɔːt/	(v)	to help someone by paying for his or her food, clothes, etc.

UNIT 6

Vocabulary	Pronunciation	Part of speech	Definition
break	/breɪk/	(n)	a stop in an activity for a short time
careless	/'keələs/	(adj)	done, made or said without paying attention
colleague	/'kɒliːg/	(n)	someone who works with you
customer	/'kʌstəmə/	(n)	someone who buys goods or services from a business
earn	/ɜːn/	(v)	to get money from doing work
find out	/faɪnd 'aʊt/	(phr v)	to get information about something
get by	/get baɪ/	(phr v)	to deal with a situation by having just enough of something
goal	/gəʊl/	(n)	something you want to do successfully in the future
look at	/lʊk ət/	(phr v)	to direct your eyes in order to see something
messy	/'mesi/	(adj)	untidy or dirty
profit	/'prɒfɪt/	(n)	money that you make from selling goods or services for more than they cost to make or provide
project	/'prɒdʒekt/	(n)	a piece of work that is for a particular purpose or a detailed study of a topic
run out	/rʌn aʊt/	(phr v)	to not have enough of something
skill	/skɪl/	(n)	the ability to do an activity or job well
spend time	/spend taɪm/	(phr)	to use time to do something

Vocabulary	Pronunciation	Part of speech	Definition
strength	/streŋθ/	(n)	a good quality or ability that makes someone good at something
stress	/stress/	(n)	feelings of worry caused by problems
take over	/teɪk 'əʊvə/	(phr v)	to replace someone or something
waste time	/weɪst taɪm/	(phr)	to use time badly
weakness	/'wiːknəs/	(n)	a quality of someone or something that is not good
write down	/raɪt daʊn/	(phr v)	to write something on a piece of paper so that you do not forget it
UNIT 7			
achievement	/ə'tʃiːvmənt/	(n)	something good and successful that you do, usually by working hard
amazing	/ə'meɪzɪŋ/	(adj)	very surprising
bored	/bɔːd/	(adj)	feeling unhappy because something is not interesting or because you have nothing to do
boring	/'bɔː.rɪŋ/	(adj)	not interesting or exciting
complicated	/'kɒmplɪkeɪtɪd/	(adj)	having a lot of different pieces, in a way that is difficult to understand
design	/dɪ'zaɪn/	(n)	the way something is planned and made
entrepreneur	/ˌɒntrəprə'nɜː/	(n)	someone who starts his or her own business
excited	/ɪk'saɪtɪd/	(adj)	feeling very happy and enthusiastic
exciting	/ɪk'saɪtɪŋ/	(adj)	making you feel very happy and enthusiastic
fascinated	/'fæsɪneɪtɪd/	(adj)	very interested
fascinating	/'fæsɪneɪtɪŋ/	(adj)	very interesting
interested	/'ɪntrəstɪd/	(adj)	not bored
interesting	/'ɪntrəstɪŋ/	(adj)	not boring
invention	/ɪn'venʃən/	(n)	something made for the first time
point	/pɔɪnt/	(n)	an opinion, fact or idea that is said or written
purpose	/'pɜːpəs/	(n)	why you do something or why something exists

Vocabulary	Pronunciation	Part of speech	Definition
relaxed	/rɪˈlækst/	(adj)	feeling happy and comfortable because nothing is worrying you
relaxing	/rɪˈlæksɪŋ/	(adj)	making you feel happy and comfortable because nothing is worrying you
remarkable	/rɪˈmɑːkəbl/	(adj)	very unusual or noticeable in a way that you admire
retire	/rɪˈtaɪə/	(v)	to leave your job and stop working, usually because you get older
simple	/ˈsɪmpl/	(adj)	made without extra things that are not needed
situation	/ˌsɪtjuˈeɪʃən/	(n)	the things that are happening and are present at a particular time and place
success	/səkˈses/	(n)	something that has a good result
surprised	/səˈpraɪzd/	(adj)	feeling or showing surprise because something has happened that you did not expect
surprising	/səˈpraɪzɪŋ/	(adj)	not expected and making someone feel surprised
tired	/taɪəd/	(adj)	in need of rest or sleep
tiring	/taɪərɪŋ/	(adj)	making you feel in need of rest or sleep
use	/juːs/	(n)	a reason why something is used

UNIT 8

Vocabulary	Pronunciation	Part of speech	Definition
alternative	/ɔːlˈtɜːnətɪv/	(n)	one of two or more things you can choose between
beyond	/biˈjɒnd/	(prep)	on the other side of something
effect	/ɪˈfekt/	(n)	a change, reaction or result that is caused by something
evaluate	/ɪˈvæljueɪt/	(v)	to consider or study something carefully to decide how good or bad it is
expert	/ˈekspɜːt/	(n)	someone who has a lot of knowledge about something
explore	/ɪkˈsplɔː/	(v)	to travel around a place to find out what is there

Vocabulary	Pronunciation	Part of speech	Definition
impact	/ˈɪmpækt/	(n)	the effect that a person, event or situation has on someone or something
issue	/ˈɪʃuː/	(n)	an important topic or problem that people are discussing
journey	/ˈdʒɜːni/	(n)	a long trip from one place to another
option	/ˈɒpʃən/	(n)	a choice
path	/pɑːθ/	(n)	the direction that a person or thing moves in
planet	/ˈplænɪt/	(n)	a large, round object in space that moves around the sun or another star
private	/ˈpraɪvɪt/	(adj)	controlled by a person or a company and not by the government
problem	/ˈprɒbləm/	(n)	a situation that causes difficulties and needs to be solved
public	/ˈpʌblɪk/	(adj)	open to everyone to see or use
reach	/riːtʃ/	(v)	to arrive somewhere
solution	/səˈluːʃən/	(n)	the answer to the problem
spacecraft	/ˈspeɪskrɑːft/	(n)	a vehicle that can travel into space
surface	/ˈsɜːfɪs/	(n)	the top or outside part of something
talent	/ˈtælənt/	(n)	a natural ability to do something

VIDEO AND AUDIO SCRIPTS

UNIT 1

The Grand Canal

This is Venice, Italy. It is full of fantastic palaces and, of course, a lot of canals.

There are 117 little islands between the canals and 400 bridges. Historically, Venice is an important city for art and business. But these days, most people know it as a popular tourist centre.

The Grand Canal is the largest canal in Venice. It's more than two miles long. It's Venice's busiest road, but you won't see cars here. Instead, you'll see a kind of boat called the gondola.

At one time, there was probably a river here, but the Grand Canal is man-made. The palaces and other buildings are on stilts – long legs that go deep into the ground under the canal.

A gondola ride takes about half an hour. It's one of the best 30 minutes you can spend in your life.

Here is the Ca' d'Oro, one of Venice's most beautiful palaces. It was built in the 15th century and was then decorated with gold.

And this is the Rialto Bridge, the oldest bridge across the Grand Canal. It's made of stone and for nearly 300 years, it was the only way to cross the Grand Canal on foot.

No wonder two of Venice's nicknames are 'The City of Bridges' and 'The Bride of the Sea'.

1.1

place
hot
quick
up

1.2

James: Welcome to the Travel Podcast. I'm James. I'm here with Suzie and today we're looking at unusual places where people actually live. Suzie, when you travelled, did you see any interesting or **strange** homes around the world?

Suzie: Well, it depends what you mean by strange. I live in a detatched house, so the **apartment** buildings in New York, for example, seem pretty strange to me.

James: I really mean places that very few people know about ...

Suzie: Oh, I see ... erm. Well, when I was on holiday last year in Peru, I saw a really old city made out of mud. You could say that is interesting.

James: Yes, that is very interesting! And so are the cave houses at a place called Matmata.

Suzie: Matmata? Is that in Egypt?

James: No, it's in Tunisia. Take a look at the picture. You might **recognize** it from the *Star Wars* films. They filmed some of the scenes there because the cave houses look strange, like maybe they aren't real. But actually, these houses in the **caves** are real. People started living in them 700 years ago. They made them out of the **rock**.

Suzie: Wow! That's **ancient**! Where is it exactly?

James: It's about 355 kilometres south of the **capital**, Tunis. I'd love to go there. Actually, when I was younger I went to Cappadocia in Turkey. It was fantastic! There are cave houses there, too. It's in Anatolia, in the centre of Turkey. Take a look.

Suzie: The buildings look like mushrooms!

James: Interesting place, isn't it? The caves formed from rock more than 8,000 years ago. People changed them into homes during the Roman period. Some people still live there now.

Suzie: Now? That's amazing. But did you know that some people live on **bridges**? Look at these two photos.

James: Oh yeah. This one is beautiful and it looks very old. It's in Italy, isn't it? Is it Rome?

Suzie: Well, it is in Italy. It's called the Ponte Vecchio, but it's actually in Florence, north of Rome. They built the bridge in 1345. There was another bridge there before, but an accident destroyed it. So they made this one and people started to live there. It's amazing, isn't it?

James: Yes, it is. But the bridge in the other picture looks newer.

Suzie: Yeah, that's Neft Dashlari in Azerbaijan.

James: Where?

Suzie: Azerbaijan. You know – A-Z-E-R-B-A-I-J-A-N.

James: Oh, of course. The bridge looks really long and it looks like it has a lot of factories. Do a lot of people work there?

Suzie: Yes, they drill for oil from under the sea there. They decided that the workers needed somewhere to live, so they built a kind of 'city' above the sea. The bridge is about 48 kilometres long. They put houses, libraries, schools and even a cinema there.

James: Really? So, hundreds of people live there?

Suzie: About 2,000 people live there. It even appeared in a *James Bond* film.

James: Well, it makes my house look really boring!

Suzie: Mine, too!

1.3

Teacher: OK, everyone. Today we are talking about interesting places.

I'd like to talk about the city of Vancouver, in British Columbia, Canada. It's one of the most beautiful cities in the world. We often think cities are **urban areas**, with **traffic** and **modern** buildings. We don't usually think cities have **woods**, **lakes** and **fields**. But Vancouver is a 'green city' – a place that's good to live in because it has clean air, water and land. Vancouver has the best parts of green forests and city life. I would like to talk about some of the history of Vancouver as well as some of the advantages and disadvantages of this 'green' city.

Vancouver originally was a place where the native people of the area lived and traded for thousands of years before Europeans came to live there in the 1800s. Then in 1886, at the first city meeting, the people of Vancouver asked the national government to give the city 1,000 acres to use as a park. They got the land from the government and started Stanley Park. This was the start of Vancouver becoming a green city with many parks and beautiful views. But being a green city with lots of parks has both advantages and disadvantages.

First of all, let's look at some of the positives. Obviously, Stanley Park is a large park. In fact, because it **is located** in the city of Vancouver, it is the third largest urban park in North America. It has many gardens, walking paths, trees and even animals, such as bald eagles, coyotes and seals. As we know, lots of trees help clean the city air. Also, lots of parks give people many places to walk, so they're healthier. Since Vancouver is near the mountains and the ocean, people can enjoy the outdoors easily during the warm, sunny summers. When people go to Stanley Park, they can enjoy ancient trees as they walk near the ocean or they can have fun by Beaver Lake, which, like Stanley Park, helps make Vancouver one of the healthiest and cleanest cities in the world.

I'd also like to talk about some disadvantages of parks in Vancouver. Space in a city is very important. Having many parks means that people have less space to build houses and apartments. Because Vancouver is located between the mountains and the ocean, there's not much room for new buildings. This makes Vancouver an expensive city. Also, when you have a beautiful place to live, a lot of people want to go there. This makes the city crowded. Actually, Vancouver has very bad traffic. Lastly, when you have a lot of parks, wild animals in the parks can sometimes be a problem. For example, Stanley Park gives information to people about what to do if they see a coyote. In my opinion, having coyotes in a city park is bad.

Finally, while I think these disadvantages might mean that some people would not want to visit Vancouver, I personally feel that most people would enjoy Vancouver. In my opinion, being close to nature and having a healthy city are worth paying a little more money for. And a lot of people agree with this idea because Vancouver is a very popular place to visit and live in. So I would recommend that people visit Vancouver and enjoy the many parks, the clean, healthy city and the interesting sights.

1.4

1 Obviously, Stanley Park is a large park.
2 In fact, because it is located in the city of Vancouver, it is the third largest urban park in North America.
3 As we know, lots of trees help clean the city air.
4 Finally, while I think these disadvantages might mean that some people would not want to visit Vancouver, ...
5 ... I personally feel that most people would enjoy Vancouver.
6 In my opinion, being close to nature and having a healthy city are worth paying a little more money for.

1.5

1 I'd like to talk about the city of Vancouver, in British Columbia, Canada.
2 First of all, let's look at some of the positives.
3 I'd also like to talk about some disadvantages of parks in Vancouver.
4 Finally, while I think these disadvantages mean that some people would not want to visit Vancouver, I personally feel that most people would enjoy Vancouver.

1.6

I'd like to talk about the city of Vancouver, in British Columbia, Canada.

1.7

First of all, let's look at some of the positives.

UNIT 2

Harbin's ice festival

Narrator: This is Harbin in China, also known as 'the Ice City'. Every winter, for over 30 years, Harbin has held an ice festival. These days tourists from all over the world come to visit.

It takes 7,000 people working together to build the ice city. There are large snow sculptures and full-size buildings.

They cut ice bricks from the frozen Songhua River. But for some sculptures they need clear bricks that look like glass. The clear bricks are made for the festival using very pure water. This stops air bubbles from freezing into the ice.

In the day time, visitors can see the snow sculptures at 'Sun Island'. They can also watch the artists at work or, for visitors who want to make their own sculptures, there are classes and competitions.

At night, the buildings of 'Ice and Snow World' light up with a rainbow of colours. There are ice castles, ice skyscrapers and ice slides, which are very popular with children.

Harbin is in the northeast of China where cold winds from Siberia bring them an average winter temperature of minus 16.8 °C – the perfect temperature to build from ice and snow. The freezing temperatures do not keep the visitors away. This year over a million people are expected to come. Besides exploring the ice city, visitors can play ice sports and games and see amazing firework shows. The festival opens on the fifth of January each year and stays open for at least four weeks and often much longer – until the spring comes and the Ice City melts away for another year.

2.1

Reporter 1: Today I'm at the Festival of Ideas, which has been held in the UK every October since 2008. It's a free festival with lots of activities, organized by the University of Cambridge. But it isn't just for students. Anyone interested in arts and science can go to the **lectures**, talks, classes and performances. The festival gets bigger and bigger every year; the first year, 7,000 people attended, but by the third year that number had almost doubled. We asked one of the visitors about the festival.

Hello, there. Can you introduce yourself and tell me, is this your first time at the festival here in Cambridge?

Judith: My name is Judith, and no, I come here every year!

Reporter 1: Can you tell us why you like coming to the festival?

Judith: Well, it's an interesting event to come to. It's great for kids and adults. I **enjoy** learning about all the new ideas people have on important topics. We don't get much time to really think or learn about new things in everyday life, but you can do exactly that at this festival.

Reporter 1: So, what kinds of things do people learn? Do people concentrate on learning just one thing?

Judith: No, most people plan on going to several events. For example, today I learnt some history. I went to a lecture about the English Civil War, which happened between 1642 and 1651. It was really interesting! Yesterday, I played games to find out about gravity. It was a science **activity**. And tomorrow, I'm going to a talk on the global economy, which I'm sure will really make me think!

Reporter 1: Are there any things you don't like about it? Are you ever bored?

Judith: Not really. The only problem is that it's really crowded!

Reporter 1: Judith, like many others, is really enjoying the Festival of Ideas. Nowadays around the world, there are many festivals, often based on nature, food or **culture**. Take the Cherry Blossom Festival in Japan, for example. In Tokyo, the capital of Japan, the cherry blossom festival is held in early April. It is an important festival celebrating nature. The actual dates change every year, because the celebration happens only when the trees have cherry blossoms. So, it is a little different from a festival that has the same date every year and it's not organized in the same way as many other festivals. Our reporter Mike Pearce went to Tokyo to find out.

Reporter 2: Today, I am talking with Yuki. She sells food during the cherry blossom festival in Ueno Park in Tokyo. Hi, Yuki.

Yuki: Hi. Welcome to the cherry blossom festival!

Reporter 2: Thanks. So, what happens here?

Yuki: Well, as you can see, it's a cherry blossom festival. It is a celebration of spring and the cherry flowers. So, it doesn't have specific activities that people do. Instead, people come to enjoy the cherry blossoms and have a picnic under the trees. We have about a thousand trees, full of beautiful flowers.

Reporter 2: Do you have many people here from other countries?

Yuki: Yes. Our visitors are from all over the world. In addition to the cherry blossoms, there are lots of food stalls and people can hire a boat to go around the lake too. There are many beautiful, natural places here. Some people prefer to visit some of the park's many museums, but I think Tokyo is one of the best places to come for the cherry blossom festival.

Reporter 2: Well, I hope you enjoy the rest of the event!

Reporter 1: Visiting such festivals is not just for **entertainment**; it's also a fantastic way to find out about the culture of a different country.

I went to Oman in the Middle East recently to do just that.

I'm here in Muscat at the festival of culture and heritage, talking to Nasrra. She is visiting the Muscat Festival with her family. The event is held in January and February each year in Oman, and Nasrra has been coming for the last couple of years. Hi, Nasrra. Are you enjoying the festival?

Nasrra: Yes! It's wonderful!

Reporter 1: Can you tell us something about the festival?

Nasrra: Of course. It's a chance for people to learn about the heritage and culture of Oman.

Reporter 1: So, why are you here?

Nasrra: My mother and father want to watch some of the sports; there was cycling last year and also a camel race. You can also learn **traditional** dance. But I decided to go to the fashion show.

Reporter 1: That sounds great.

Nasrra: Yeah. And after we finish watching the races and shows, we'll go and eat some traditional food.

Reporter 1: Sounds amazing! I hope you all have a great time.

So these international festivals, with lots of music, food and fashion, are providing a different type of experience for people. Next week, we'll be looking at ...

2.2

Well, it's an interesting event to come to.

2.3

1 So, what kinds of things do people learn?
2 Are there any things you don't like about it?
3 Do you have many people here from other countries?

2.4

1 Do you like your job?
2 Are you a chef?
3 What time does the festival start?
4 What kinds of food do you have?
5 Is it all good?
6 Where do people eat their lunch?
7 Do you like the food?
8 Is the work interesting?

2.5

Ali: Paul, you have cousins in the US, don't you? What's your opinion? Which is the best North American holiday or celebration?

Paul: Hmm. Well, I like Independence Day in the US because of the **fireworks** and New Year's Eve often has fireworks, too. But I think the best holiday is Thanksgiving.

Ali: Why do you like Thanksgiving?

Paul: Everyone has something to be thankful for, so everyone can **celebrate** it. Both the US and Canada celebrate it.

Ali: Really? How do people celebrate it?

Paul: Well, most people get together with family and friends and have a big meal.

Ali: What do they eat?

Paul: They usually eat a traditional meal. This is usually a delicious turkey with stuffing for the main **dish**. You should try it! Most traditional Thanksgiving meals have food which is from the Americas, like potatoes, corn and cranberries. For dessert, they eat pumpkin pie, but some people prefer different kinds of pie, like apple.

Ali: Is the food the same in both countries?

Paul: Actually, there are some differences in the food. In Canada, for example, the pumpkin pie is spicy, but in the US it's sweet. I like the American style, with whipped cream. You have to try it! Another dish which is different is the stuffing. For instance, in Canada stuffing is often made from rice or bread, but in the southern US it could be made from cornbread. In the eastern US, sometimes oysters are used in the stuffing.

Ali: That all sounds delicious. Are there any special decorations for Thanksgiving?

Paul: Well, people often **decorate** their dinner tables and homes with things such as colourful leaves, autumn vegetables and candles. The decorations usually have autumn colours, like red, yellow and orange.

Ali: Do people give **gifts** or do some special activities?

Paul: Well, people don't really give gifts, but there are some special activities. For example, both countries celebrate with **parades** with marching bands and people in **costumes**. It's also traditional to watch sport on TV.

ALi: It sounds like the celebration is almost the same in both countries.

Paul: Well, there are some differences between Canadian and American Thanksgiving.

Ali: Like what?

Paul: Well, for instance, in Canada, the holiday is celebrated on the second Monday in October. But in the US it's on the fourth Thursday in November. Another difference is that in Canada people enjoy small, local parades. In the US they have a huge parade in New York City and people all over the US watch it on TV.

People in the New York parade sometimes wear costumes. One last difference is that each country has different reasons for the holiday. In Canada the holiday celebrates the autumn harvest. But Americans celebrate the autumn harvest and remembering the Native Americans helping settlers hunt and grow food.

Ali: That sounds like a lot of fun. I want to go to a Thanksgiving celebration in both countries!

2.6

1 ... some people prefer different kinds of pie, like apple.

2 ... people often decorate their dinner tables and homes with things such as colourful leaves, autumn vegetables and candles.

3 For example, both countries celebrate with parades with marching bands and people in costumes.

4 Well, for instance, in Canada, the holiday is celebrated on the second Monday in October.

UNIT 3

Fibre optic cables

In the middle of the ocean, deep underwater, violent volcanic activity changes the ocean floor.

Usually we don't know anything about this – until the internet stops working.

99% of all internet traffic between continents goes through cables at the bottom of the ocean.

But sometimes there are problems. For example, ten years ago nine important fibre optic cables on the ocean floor between Taiwan and the Philippines suddenly went dead.

Computers all over Asia crashed. Engineers looked for the problem and they found that the cables were broken.

Volcanic activity caused heavy rocks to move and break the cables.

Suddenly, many people in Southeast Asia couldn't use the internet. What would happen to businesses? It took weeks to find and repair the cables.

Engineers used this special ship, called the Wave Sentinel. Its job is to keep the internet connected.

3.1

disabled
fish
kitchen
suit
pollution
save
shave
watch
wash

3.2

1 station
2 sort
3 short
4 wish
5 which
6 robots
7 match
8 ocean
9 accident
10 cheap

3.3

1 sorts
2 cheap
3 wash
4 sea
5 shave

3.4

Host: Welcome to University Radio, the station run by students for students. I'm Chen Hu and this is *Science Today*. Our subject is technological development and our guest is Professor Joanne Kent, expert in robotics. Thanks for coming in, Professor. When we think of **robots**, we generally think of science fiction films. Is this out of date?

Professor: Yes, it is. Technology has **developed** very fast over the last ten years and robots are part of everyday life. Robots can now do many important things.

Host: What kinds of things?

Professor: Well, they have been used in factories for years; Japan and China have the most industrial robots in the world. But now robots are coming into our lives in other ways. In Japan, Thailand and Hong Kong, for example, there are robot waiters in restaurants and in South Korea a robot is used as an English teacher. Robots weren't used very much in the past, since they were always really expensive. But because they have become cheaper, they are being used in new and interesting ways. One key area is the way robots can help with medical care.

Host: Can you explain that a little more?

Professor: Well, a good example is the robotic **suit** for **disabled** people. Robots can now assist people who can't walk. They can help them to move again. People 'wear' the robot, like clothes. The robot then helps move the person's arms or legs. For example, one man, Joey Abbica, couldn't walk because of an **accident** at work three years earlier. Before the accident, Joey could surf really well. In fact, he won lots of competitions, but after the accident he couldn't walk at all. He wasn't even able to sit up on his own when a visitor came. And he couldn't even feel his legs when doctors touched them. But when he put on the robotic suit, he was able to stand up and walk on his own again. He isn't able to walk at all without the suit. Robotics changed his life.

Host: So people have a much better quality of life, thanks to these new types of robots?

Professor: Yes, that's right. Service robots are also very helpful to people.

Host: What do service robots do?

Professor: Well, one of the reasons that service robots were invented is to save people time. They do all the jobs around the house that people find difficult, dirty or boring. For instance, robots can put clothes into a washing machine, and plates and cups into a dishwasher and they can clean your kitchen and bathroom. But for some people, service robots are really important; they're not just a **luxury**. Elderly people, for example, can't always do housework easily. They might need help from robots. The robot means they are able to stay in their own homes for longer.

Host: So, robots can help people in their everyday life, but how do they help more generally?

Professor: Robots are now solving modern problems, too. Have you heard of robotic fish?

Host: I haven't, but I assume they are robots that swim in water. What do they do?

Professor: They were developed to help scientists with information collection. They look like fish, they swim and move like other fish, but when they are swimming, they can **collect information** about the amount of pollution in the water. Scientists can find out about pollution quickly, due to the robotic fish.

Host: Well, we've heard of robots that clean your house, so it's good to know they can help keep the environment clean, too. OK, we have some questions coming in, so let's hear the first one ...

3.5

1 You will hear the main ideas and some additional information.

2 You will hear the main ideas as well as some additional information.

3.6

News reporter: For a long time, people have asked the same question: Do computers stop us from learning and developing? Do they make us **stupid**? A recent study at Columbia University in New York looked at this question, in particular how computers affect our **memory**. They wanted to find out if computers have changed the way we remember information.

First, the scientists did **research** on what happens when people are asked **difficult** questions. They found that what we think when we hear difficult questions has changed because of websites like Google™. When people were asked difficult questions in the past, scientists believe they tried to think of the answer to the question. However, because of modern technology, the first thing people think about now is how to find the answer; they don't try to answer it themselves. For example, they think about what they might put into Google™, but in the past they thought about the question itself.

Second, scientists found that computers have changed the type of information we remember. There are advantages and disadvantages to these changes. A disadvantage is that it seems that people now forget facts, especially if they know the information will be saved in a **file**. On the other hand, an advantage is that they remember the **location** of the fact: in other words, where to find it. In one test, scientists told university students some facts and also where the facts were saved in a file. Most of the students couldn't remember the facts, but they were able to remember the files and the location of the facts.

In conclusion, it seems that computers are not making us stupid, but they are making us lazy! Scientists believe that we are spending time remembering where and how we can find things, but we're not trying to remember the information itself anymore.

3.7

1 When people were asked difficult questions in the past, scientists believe they tried to think of the answer to the question. However, because of modern technology, the first thing people think about now is how to find the answer ...

2 For example, they think about what they might put into Google™, but in the past they thought about the question itself.

3 ... it seems that people now forget facts, especially if they know the information will be saved in a file. On the other hand, an advantage is they remember the location of the fact: in other words, where to find it.

4 In conclusion, it seems that computers are not making us stupid, but they are making us lazy!

UNIT 4

The impact of oceans on climate

Water covers almost 70% of the Earth. But it doesn't just stay in the same place.

Like the air above it, the water in the oceans moves around the planet. It moves because the Earth is spinning and this has a big effect on our climate.

The spinning of the Earth causes large circles of currents in the oceans. These circular currents are called 'ocean gyres'. North of the equator, they move clockwise. South of the equator, they move in the opposite direction. These gyres move water and heat. That's why they are important to our climate.

Ocean currents move lots of energy and heat away from the equator. This changes our climate. For example, warmer water from the equator moves thousands of miles north. The result is warmer weather there.

South of the equator, ocean gyres are also important. They move cooler water north along the west coast of Chile in South America.

This water has lots of food in it, so it's a perfect place for fish to live. In fact, 20% of the fish we catch for food comes from this small part of the ocean.

Without these ocean gyres, our world would be a very different place.

4.1

1 **A:** Did you know global warming is still increasing?
B: Is it?

2 **A:** It's my birthday today.
B: Really? Happy birthday!

3 **A:** The weather got really chilly, didn't it?
B: I suppose so.

4 **A:** Thanks for inviting me to your party!
B: You're welcome. It'll be nice to see you!

5 **A:** Dinner was great.
B: Good. Glad you liked it.

4.2

Sergio: So we need to think of some questions for this survey about the weather, Murat. Should we make a list of them?

Murat: I think we should decide what we want to find out. Professor Hadland told us we should look at all the different things we could survey, group them and then try to choose the most important ones.

Sergio: Right. Effects of weather on mood.

Murat: Well, we're looking at weather in northern Europe where it is often cold and wet. Generally, in northern Europe people see sunshine as positive, which I find strange. In my country, it's hot all the time, so we like **cool** days. But anyway ... I read some research about weather and moods in Sweden. I really enjoyed reading it, but it had so many different answers it wasn't clear that weather changes people's mood.

Sergio: Oh ... great ...

Murat: But they did find *some* specific results. They noticed that good, **dry**, sunny weather didn't make people happier. But bad weather made people more **upset**, if they were already unhappy.

Sergio: And ... ?

Murat: And, therefore, unhappy people felt even worse when it was wet and windy.

Sergio: Oh, OK. So for the 'good weather' category – no link. But for the 'bad weather' part – it causes unhappy people to feel worse.

Murat: Yes. And the amount of sunlight seems to be linked to feeling tired. When it is sunny, people have more **energy** and are less tired. So they like doing more things outside.

Sergio: OK, I've added that.

Murat: Also, I read something about **humid** weather. Another experiment showed that really humid weather changes how people work. When it is humid, they might plan to study at a different time. Or maybe they might stop studying and take a break when they begin having difficulties. As a result, it is more difficult to work and it's hard to pay attention. And there was something about heat and anger. Really hot weather can make people angrier, I think.

Sergio: Are you sure? Should I add it?

Murat: Well, write it down anyway.

Sergio: OK, which area do you think we should look at then?

Murat: I think the humid one is important. Especially for students.

Sergio: But the one on bad weather making people feel worse could be interesting, too; it sounds like there are more useful facts with that topic.

Murat: Yes, true. I'm not sure about the really hot weather and being **angry**; I can't remember if that's true. So let's leave that out. That leaves three possible topics – humid weather stops us working, sunny weather makes us less tired or bad weather makes people feel worse.

Sergio: Hmm, the one about humid weather looks at how people study. It isn't really about how people feel, so it isn't useful for us. I'd go with bad weather or sunny weather.

Murat: I see what you mean. We could choose either of those. I'm not sure about the bad weather one. It's a bit depressing, isn't it? Which do you **prefer**?

Sergio: I don't really care.

Murat: Well, if you don't care, let's do the one about sunshine and having energy. It's more positive.

4.3

Murat: ... and so I put all the results into a spreadsheet on my laptop. Here are all the answers from the surveys I did, 12 of them. Oh and the three surveys that you did.

Sergio: OK ... let's see what they say.

Murat: We asked how people felt when they woke up on a sunny day.

Sergio: And?

Murat: Fourteen out of fifteen people said they feel better in sunny weather than when it is very wet or rainy. They prefer sunshine.

Sergio: OK.

Murat: And 13 of them said it made them feel they could get a lot done that day. Also, 12 out of 15 people said that they did more when the weather was good.

Sergio: What about when they feel most tired?

Murat: Well, everyone said that they felt tired if the weather was cloudy and dark. And 14 said they had the most energy when there was lots of light.

Sergio: So, good weather means that people have more energy.

Murat: Yeah, that is what our survey seems to show. Of course, it might be different in another country. Maybe it depends on the place you live.

4.4

Reporter: Global warming is an important issue around the world. Recently it has created problems in the Western Ghats rainforests of India. Forests are important for slowing down global warming because of the work that trees do for us. Trees are global cleaners. They take in carbon dioxide (CO_2), the gas that heats the atmosphere. So, we keep making global warming worse every time we cut down trees. Then global warming continues to damage the forest. More trees **disappear** because the changes in temperature stop the normal growth of the forest. Nowadays, rainforests get less rain and this is changing the way they work.

Governments around the world are beginning to work on the problem. Although governments say they will stop people damaging the forests, scientists don't think the work is happening quickly enough. The scientists say the forests are changing. The animals, and the plants that animals need, are changing. In fact, scientists **believe** 45% of the forest areas are going to change completely in the next 80 years.

This is where the purple frog **becomes** important. A report tells us that the frog is in danger of disappearing forever. The frog can run very fast, makes a noise like a small chicken and is one of the most **unusual** animals in the world. Of course, for some people, the end of one type of frog is not important. But it is for Sathyabhama Das Biju, a researcher from Delhi University who **discovered** it in 2003. For him, the problems of the purple frog show what global warming is doing to the Indian rainforests. He explains that this interesting animal won't be around much longer if we don't **look after** the forests.

Biju is going to present information about the forests next week. He hopes to get people interested in saving this frog and other animals that live in rainforests. During the next week, many people are meeting to talk about the climate and **saving** the rainforests. According to Biju, we need to plan now or we will probably lose some species completely. If we don't think **carefully** about the climate of the forests, the purple frog possibly won't be around for much longer. On to the weather report now ...

4.5

1 It is more difficult to work in high humidity, so our concentration drops.
2 People have more energy in sunny weather. Therefore, they can get a lot done if the sun is shining.
3 Some countries are really hot and don't get much rain. As a result, there isn't enough water for people to drink.

UNIT 5

Kasparov versus Deep Blue

Narrator: Humans began playing chess in northern India nearly 1,500 years ago. But we only recently began competing against computers. Garry Kasparov is one of the greatest world chess champions in history. In the 1990s, he played a famous match against an IBM super computer. The computer's name was Deep Blue. To play chess well, you need many different skills. But computers can only calculate numbers. Kasparov started the first game. An engineer from IBM moved the chess pieces for Deep Blue. A chess genius like Kasparov can think about three moves a second. But in that same second, the computer is able to process 200 million possible moves. Garry Kasparov played the first game very well. It took nearly four hours. In the end, the computer lost.

Commentator: And Garry Kasparov has won the first game against Deep Blue in fantastic style.

Narrator: But the second game was different. Kasparov tried to trick Deep Blue into a mistake. But the computer didn't make a move. It was quiet for 15 minutes. It seemed like the computer was thinking. It wasn't tricked. Instead, it made a great move of its own. This time the human was losing to the machine. Kasparov tried to escape, but he couldn't. For the first time in history, a computer beat the world chess champion.

Commentator: And Kasparov has resigned.

5.1

1 The teacher's name isn't Mr Rosso. It's Mr Rosson.

2 I had a golf lesson, not a tennis lesson.

3 The match is at 6:00 tonight, not 6:30, so don't be late.

4 Yasmin doesn't do Drama classes, she does Gymnastics classes.

5 The competition will be in Colombia, not in Brazil.

5.2

Amina: For my project I looked at some unusual sports that people play around the world. These aren't team sports. Instead people compete to win individually. I'd like to start by talking about 'chess boxing'. You may already know about the two sports. Chess is a game played with a board and different chess pieces. Very intelligent people often play this game because players need to think very carefully. Boxing is a totally different kind of sport, though. Being **strong** is more important because boxers have to hit each other. They wear gloves and helmets in the ring, but it's still difficult. Now, chess boxing is a new type of sport, where the players do both activities. They start with boxing, sorry, I mean chess and then do some boxing, and they continue doing each activity back and forth – alternating. The person who wins the boxing match or the chess game first is the **champion**. One benefit of this sport is that it gives people a chance to **compete** physically and mentally. It isn't just thinking or physical activity; it's both.

Another sport that challenges people is urban golf. Urban golf is similar to normal golf, but you don't need to go to a golf course. You get clubs and a golf ball – well, actually, it's a soft tennis ball instead of a hard golf ball. Then you can play in the street, which is why it's called 'urban'. If you play urban golf, you don't need to go anywhere special or need much money to play. You just agree where you want to **hit** the ball, for example, at a sign in the street or a rubbish bin. On the other hand, **intelligent** players know that you may break something if you hit the ball too hard, so they try to play fairly carefully.

Next, I'd like to talk about the Moroccan desert footrace, which is also called the *Marathon des Sables* or the Sahara Marathon. This race is held every year over a week or rather over six days. The runners have to be really strong. On the longest day, the runners have to run 92 kilometres. The best thing about it is that the champion can say he, or she, has won the hardest marathon in the world.

Finally, I'd like to look at sepak takraw. This is a type of volleyball and is very popular in Southeast Asia. The players use a different kind of ball and they can use their feet to **kick** the ball or hit it with their knees, chest or head. The sport began in Indonesia and it – no, not Indonesia – it began in Malaysia, although it is also very popular in Thailand and Indonesia. One good thing about sepak takraw is that it is now played in schools in many countries, including Japan and gets children to play sport.

5.3

1 Now, chess boxing is a new type of sport where the players do both activities. They start with boxing, sorry, I mean chess and then do some boxing and they continue doing each activity back and forth – alternating.

2 Urban golf is similar to normal golf, but you don't need to go to a golf course. You get clubs and a golf ball – well, actually, it's a soft tennis ball instead of a hard golf ball.

3 Next, I'd like to talk about the Moroccan desert footrace, which is also called the *Marathon des Sables* or the Sahara Marathon. This race is held every year over a week or rather over six days.

4 Finally, I'd like to look at sepak takraw. This is a type of volleyball and is very popular in Southeast Asia. The players use a different kind of ball and they can use their feet to kick the ball or hit it with their knees, chest or head. The sport began in Indonesia and it – no, not Indonesia – it began in Malaysia, although it is also very popular in Thailand and Indonesia.

5.4

Ian: Andre, I know you played in a university football team in the US, so I'd like to ask your opinion about something. Do you think the Olympic athletes, and other athletes, like football and tennis players, are too focused on getting money from companies? I went on holiday in the US last year and every time I turned on the TV, I saw a famous athlete in an advert for some product. Those athletes are getting paid a huge amount of money to be in adverts. It seems like the athletes are more interested in making money than in representing their countries. I think there is definitely more marketing and business in sport than ever before. As a long-time sport **fan**, I really think all this money and advertising from big companies is taking something away from sports and **competitions**.

Andre: Well, I would say that all athletes, even the rich and famous ones, are still very focused on the sport. Without the sport, they have no job! And athletes who aren't famous or are only a little famous, deserve to make all the money they can. Many athletes devote their whole lives to training. How can they live, work and pay for coaching all by themselves? Being an athlete, especially one who doesn't get paid, is extremely expensive. The **cost** of training is really high and athletes need to spend a lot of time training to be good at a sport.

So big companies might give money to sports teams and individual athletes to help them train. In some competitions, like the Olympics, there are both professional players and amateurs – you know, people who do the sport as a hobby, and not as a job. I think both should be able to get **support** from companies. Look at Novak Djokovic. He's a Serbian tennis player who is paid money by a clothing company to wear their clothes and be in their adverts. Other companies support him, too. Without all the help from companies, he might not have enough money to play tennis as his 'job'. Having that time and money allows him to be such a good tennis player!

Ian: But when a big company pays a team or an athlete, it makes them wear the company name and designs and they sign contracts ... isn't that really like being an employee and working for a company? To me, these athletes work in advertising and marketing!

Andre: You have a point, but if the athletes don't get good coaching, they might not **score** a lot of points and do well in competitions. If that happens, they can lose their chance to make a lot of money after the competitions are over. And actually, only about five percent of Olympic athletes get money from big companies to be in adverts.

Ian: That doesn't sound fair. Shouldn't countries pay their own athletes a **salary** to train? After all, they do represent the countries. I read that in the UK, the government pays the country's Olympic athletes to train, so there is less pressure there to get money from a company. Also, there are **prizes** for all the competitions and sometimes that gives them extra money.

Andre: Well, a lot of countries can't pay the costs for training athletes. And of course, the countries with lots of money can train their athletes very well. If companies are supporting lots of athletes, more people can participate in competitions.

Ian: Still, I think all this money takes something away from the Olympics and other sporting events. We see adverts almost everywhere!

Andre: But being in an advert is a great opportunity for the athlete and the business. If an athlete lets his or her face be on a cereal box or wears some clothing with a company's name on it, people will probably buy the product. So it's good for the company and the athlete gets more money to train. I also think that all the adverts at big competitions like the Olympics or the World Cup help lower the ticket prices for fans, so the competitions don't have to **charge** so much. It's good for everyone!

Ian: Hmm ... I'm not sure if I agree with you, but I understand your point.

5.5

1 I think there is definitely more marketing and business in sport than ever before.

2 And actually, only about five percent of Olympic athletes get money from big companies to be in adverts.

3 And of course, the countries with lots of money can train their athletes very well.

UNIT 6

Food in coffee shops

Narrator: Starbucks and Costa Coffee are two of the biggest coffee shop chains in the world. But in England, Caffè Nero is growing quickly and has now opened up its first American stores in Boston, Massachusetts.

Gerry Ford: We didn't look at Costa or Starbucks and try to mimic them at all or do anything similar. And, for better or for worse, we kind of marched to our own drum.

Narrator: Gerry Ford started Caffè Nero in London, but his stores use an Italian model. Coffee is the most important item, but coffee shops only really do well if they can get their customers to spend money on food, like sandwiches and cookies.

Gerry Ford: The driving force is the core product of coffee and the craftsmanship and the quality that goes into that, but the food sort of complements that. We have 30% of our sales, um, are in food, which is higher than either of the other two major brands and higher than most local independents.

Narrator: Lunchtime at Caffè Nero stores is always busy. At the London headquarters, food consultant Ursula Ferrigno helps Caffè Nero give their food some real Italian flavour. But what kind of food do customers want the most? In the end, this British company has found a successful business model selling Americanized Italian food and good quality coffee.

6.1

1 forty-eight percent

2 a half / one half

3 a fifth / one fifth

4 thirty-one point five

5 one hundred and three / one oh three

6 one thousand, five hundred and forty

7 six thousand and one

8 nought point nought one

6.2

Prof. Gould: OK, Alika. Should we look at your **project** now?

Alika: Yes, OK.

Prof. Gould: You've done a lot of reading for this, which is great. I can see you wrote a lot of information down.

Alika: Yes, but I haven't finished yet – I ran out of time. But I read as much as I could – about 103 different reports. I took part in the discussions on this with students from my study group. I studied the way people work.

Prof. Gould: Good. Can you tell me what you learnt?

Alika: Well, I looked at how people **spend time** at work. I was interested in how people **wasted time** and why they didn't work hard at their jobs; I mean, the reasons why they didn't focus on their work. I found out a lot of interesting information. For example, almost half of the workers wasted time on the internet. They were surfing the internet or writing personal emails. It was 48% of workers, in fact. 31.5% also said they spent time talking to **colleagues** instead of working. And a little under half that amount, 15%, said they took longer coffee and lunch **breaks** than they should. Only 5% said they spent time texting friends and making plans for after work.

Prof. Gould: Good. And did you find out the reasons why?

Alika: Yes. Approximately half said they didn't work hard because they weren't happy in their jobs.

Prof. Gould: I see.

Alika: And about a third, 33.5%, thought they didn't **earn** a good enough salary. They said they didn't have enough money for holidays or nice clothes. They had just enough money to get by, so they didn't work as hard as they could. Some people, about 19%, said they had to work too many hours.

Prof. Gould: So, what are some effects of people not working very hard?

Alika: Hmm ... if people aren't working hard, companies don't get what they are paying for.

Prof. Gould: Can you give me some examples?

Alika: Well, when people don't work hard, productivity goes down. Because productivity depends on how fast workers make things or provide services, if workers are not working hard, the company doesn't make a **profit**. Then they can't pay higher salaries.

6.3

Joe: Hi, Sam. Good to see you again.

Sam: Hello, Joe.

Joe: So, last time we met we talked about your business **goals**. Was it useful?

Sam: Useful? ... Yeah, it was. You really made me think! But now I have a lot of **stress** about losing money.

Joe: Oh, yes? What is making you stressed about that?

Sam: Well, I realized how many **weaknesses** a business can have! One **careless** mistake and I could lose a lot of money.

Joe: Exactly! But there are things you think will cause you to lose money?

Sam: Well, when we looked at the company's **strengths** and weaknesses, we talked about the quality and happiness of my workers, the costs of running the business and reaching new **customers** to help grow the business. Each of these areas could be a way to help make money, or a way to lose money if you don't have a good plan.

Joe: Wow – that's great! Those are all important to think about. Is there anything else?

Sam: And what else was there? Oh, of course, customers!

Joe: Well, that gives us plenty to talk about today! So, let's think about what you can do for your employees. You said that your workers were unhappy and not working hard enough. Keeping your employees happy will make them more likely to work hard for the business. Try organizing some social events once a month during work hours. That could be a good first step! Also, maybe you should paint the walls a brighter colour. The office is really dark and people feel like they're in a cave. Brighter colours can help make people happier. And happier employees will also work harder.

Sam: Oh, OK. Well, that's good to know.

Joe: You also have to cut costs. You spend far too much money on electricity every month. Turn off the lights and computers at the end of the workday. You should also find some cheaper parts for your products, which are still well made. It's a tough job, but I can help you find them.

Sam: I see. That would be great!

Joe: If you spend less money, you can make a better profit. You have some excellent adverts. But you mentioned that you are having trouble reaching new customers and growing your number of customers is really important for a successful business. So if I were you, I would try adding online sales to get more customers.

Sam: Yeah, I like that idea. I have a website already, but it looks pretty old and **messy**.

Joe: But there are things we can work on. If you want to sell online, you should start by making sure that the website doesn't look messy. If you don't have the **skills** to make it look neat, hire a professional web designer! You want a neat, clean website. It isn't something you want to be careless with.

Sam: I see. Well, I would like to have a lot of black on the website. I think that colour is professional and serious-looking.

Joe: I understand. But I think if you want to make the website attractive, it needs more colour. More colour could help the design pop out a bit more and prevent customers from leaving the website before buying anything.

Sam: Uh-huh ... That's a good idea. I actually like blue, too. I think someone else told me about colours people prefer, but I forgot.

Joe: Yes. It's easy to forget to think about something as simple as colour. The web designer you hire might have some good ideas about which colours to use. So, for our next meeting, you should create your website design and bring a plan. You could think about how it looks, as well as what it says. You don't want it to look ... well, you would want to be sure it looks well organized and the best it can be. It should also be really easy to use. Next time we'll go over your design and see how to make it better. We will also think about hiring a good web designer to make your website look great and be easy to use.

Sam: OK, great! I'll do that and bring it in next week.

6.4

Joe: Hi, Sam. Good to see you again.

Sam: Hello, Joe.

Joe: So, last time we met we talked about your business goals. Was it useful?

Sam: Useful? ... Yeah, it was. You really made me think! But now I have a lot of stress about losing money.

Joe: Oh, yes? What is making you stressed about that?

Sam: Well, I realized how many weaknesses a business can have! One careless mistake and I could lose a lot of money.

Joe: Exactly! But there are things you think will cause you to lose money?

Sam: Well, when we looked at the company's strengths and weaknesses, we talked about the quality and happiness of my workers, the costs of running the business and reaching new customers to help grow the business. Each of these areas could be a way to help make money, or a way to lose money if you don't have a good plan.

Joe: Wow – that's great! Those are all important to think about. Is there anything else?

6.5

Joe: Exactly! But there are things you think will cause you to lose money?

6.6

a Was it useful?
b Exactly! But there are things you think will cause you to lose money?
c Oh, yes?
d Well, when we look at the company's strengths and weaknesses ...
e What is making you stressed about that?
f Useful? ... Yeah, it was.

UNIT 7

Trash artists

Narrator: Kiwayu Island is located off the coast of Kenya in the Indian Ocean. There aren't many tourists on these beautiful beaches. The people who live here seem very isolated from the rest of the world. But they are actually connected to the rest of the world in a surprising way. Plastic and other trash from around the Indian Ocean washes up onto the beach daily. So every day the women of Kiwayu go to the beach to pick up trash. Why? To earn a living. They collect flip-flops and bring them to their villages. There, artists and craftsmen turn the trash into colourful ornaments and souvenirs to sell. The people of Kiwayu make good money this way. They send most of their ornaments to Nairobi, the capital of Kenya. These are then exported to stores around the world or sold on the internet.

Woman: Some people here didn't have houses before, but now they do. Some people didn't have animals for food, but now they do. Now we can buy a lot of things. Some of us couldn't send our children to school, but now we can. That's the most important thing for me.

7.1

Student presenter: Hello, everyone. So in this presentation I'd like to discuss the designers of some everyday objects: Arne Jacobsen, Sir James Dyson and Sir Jonathan Ive. These people designed **simple** things that have changed our lives and how we do everyday things. Today we are going to think about these inventors and designers, their **achievements** and how their **inventions** and **designs** have helped us.

I would like to start with Arne Jacobsen, who was born in Denmark in 1902. When he was a child, he loved to paint, but his father thought being an artist wasn't a good career. So Jacobsen became a designer of many things, including buildings and furniture. For example, here is a chair he designed in 1958. It's called the 'Egg chair'. Have any of you seen this kind of chair before?

Razia: I have. Did they call it the egg chair because of its shape? It's an interesting design.

Student presenter: Yes, you have a good **point**. I think it was called that because of the egg-like shape. Nowadays, we still see Jacobsen's designs around us. When you look at the chair design, can you guess what Jacobsen was like as a person?

Razia: His chair looks like a simple, neat design. So maybe he liked simple and neat things and not **complicated** things.

Student presenter: Actually, that's right. He did. For example, when he was growing up, he painted his room white because he didn't like all the flowers on the wallpaper he had. And as an adult, he worked hard to make his designs perfect. In fact, he often kept his workers at work until late, trying to make things better. But even though he worked hard, Jacobsen liked to joke and do funny things. For instance, as a child he liked to play jokes on others and as an adult he once wore a melon for a hat when someone dared him to. He also liked working on his own projects in his free time and found painting to be relaxing. These days, Jacobsen is famous for his modern, simple designs. His work showed that he thought about the **purpose** that his designs would serve for people.

Next, I'd like to talk about an inventor, James Dyson. Can anyone think of something you often use that might have his last name, Dyson, on it?

Razia: I know, a vacuum cleaner!

Ebru: Or a hand dryer?

Student presenter: Both of those things are correct. Dyson's designs and inventions are made to solve problems. His ideas come because he sees things that could work better, like the vacuum cleaner and hand dryer. But how did he start? Well, Dyson was born in England in 1947. His father died when he was only nine. As a result, Dyson ended up becoming someone who never gave up. He studied Art and Design before he studied Engineering. When he saw something that didn't work well, he got frustrated and worked to improve it. For example, his first invention was a wheelbarrow with a ball for a wheel. This made it easier to carry heavy things in the garden and over rough ground. It was an interesting new **use** for a ball. Also, even though he changed subjects, he was still interested in art as well as designing. Take a look at this photo. What do you see?

Ebru: It looks like a waterfall made from glass and water, with the water running up instead of falling down. That's surprising.

Student presenter: That's right. This was a piece of art that Dyson made in 2003, called *Wrong Garden*. It tricks the eye. This shows Dyson's love of good design as well as being an inventor. Dyson is still inventing new things. But he is also interested in supporting education for students, and gives money to schools to help students study so they might become inventors, too. He has even donated money to the University of Cambridge to support students and research there, with a focus on technology.

Now, I have one last picture to show you. It's a phone with a special design. It's called the iPhone. I think a lot of us know about this phone. It was designed by Sir Jonathan Ive for Apple. He is responsible for a lot of Apple's product designs, which are simple, clean and slim. Ive has won a lot of awards for his Apple designs and you can see a lot of his work in museums, too. He is from London and he was made a Knight Commander of the British Empire in 2012 for his design work. He is known as being hard-working and creative. I think that his designs will continue to influence the way we live and work for a long time!

7.2

Yasmin: Hello.

Luisa: Hi, Yasmin. It's Luisa.

Yasmin: Hi, Luisa! How are you?

Luisa: OK, I guess. Actually, I'm not that great.

Yasmin: Oh, no! What's up? Is something wrong?

Luisa: It's the presentation for our course. You know, the one on **remarkable** people who have done something really interesting or unusual. I'm having trouble doing it. Have you finished it yet?

Yasmin: Yes, almost. I just have to write a conclusion.

Luisa: Good for you. I bet it's really good.

Yasmin: Thanks, Luisa. I'm pretty happy with it, but the introduction's not great. It needs a little more work. How much have you done?

Luisa: Well ... I haven't done all of it ...

Yasmin: All? Or any of it?

Luisa: I'm not very good at finding things to present. I'm having trouble thinking of ideas. Who did you do yours on?

Yasmin: I chose Sima Najjar. She's a remarkable woman.

Luisa: Who's she? Why are you interested in her?

Yasmin: Well, she's from Jordan. She was working in fashion. She used to be the head of a modelling company before and she worked with female Arab clothing designers. So, she has had a lot of **success**. But she is famous because she started a website with videos in Arabic showing people how to do things and, without even marketing the videos, they started getting one million views a month!

Luisa: How did she do that?

Yasmin: Well, the videos are based on what people are searching for the most online. They are often about fashion, food, health, parenting and art. Many of the people who view her videos are Saudi Arabian women. Another interesting thing is that she is a mother who is working full-time. Some of her videos help other mothers to have better health after they have their babies.

Luisa: That's great that she has become really successful. Is there anything else about her life or her company that's **amazing**?

Yasmin: When her company started, most of the videos were made by people in their 20s. Nowadays, she has three full-time workers making videos. She says that as her company gets bigger, she wants to start hiring others to make videos, too. This will help more people get jobs. That's important because a lot of young people in her area don't have enough work. So, she's an **entrepreneur**, a company leader and a working mother.

Luisa: That's amazing! Wow ... I need to find someone like that.

Yasmin: Why don't you do something on Yoshiro Nakamatsu? Do you know about him?

Luisa: Umm ... I don't know a lot about Yoshiro ... who ... ?

Yasmin: Nakamatsu. Well, he was born in Japan. He is now over 90 years old and he is still an inventor.

Luisa: Umm ... his life doesn't sound that extraordinary.

Yasmin: He has created more than 3,000 inventions, including a chair that is supposed to help you think better. Some of his inventions are a bit odd, like a pair of shoes made for jumping, and glasses in the shape of eyes so that other people can't see them. He even made fake hair that can help keep you safe from others. I think Nakamatsu's **situation** is a little different from some inventors, because not everyone agrees that he has that many real inventions, but he does have a lot. Also, he didn't **retire** even after he reached the age of 80. You might want to look up more information about him online.

Luisa: OK ... I'll check him out.

Yasmin: Do you know what the teacher wants us to present?

Luisa: Well, I'm not sure I understand everything ...

7.3

1 I'm pretty happy with it.
2 She's a remarkable woman.
3 That's amazing!
4 I'll check him out.

7.4

My presentation is about Thomas Edison. He was an American inventor and he was born in 1847. He is a remarkable person because he invented a lot of the things we know and use every day, such as the electric light bulb. Well, he wasn't the first to invent one, but he *was* the first person to invent one that could last a long time. This was in 1879 while he was working in his research lab in Menlo Park, New Jersey, in the US. It lasted 13.5 hours! Another important example of Edison's amazing inventions is the motion picture camera. We all know this today as the video camera. Edison and his team invented it in 1891 and they showed short six-minute films. Equally important was Edison's work with Henry Ford, who started the Ford Motor Company. Edison was worried about America's dependence on foreign rubber for tyres. So while he was working at a lab in Florida in 1927, he found a new source of rubber in local plants ...

UNIT 8

Empire of the sun

Narrator: Here in the Mojave Desert in California, NASA, America's space agency, communicates with the spacecraft Voyager. Project scientist Dr Edward Stone became part of the Voyager team before it began its journey in 1977. Voyager's goal was to fly by the planets Jupiter, Saturn, Uranus and Neptune and to send back information to the Earth.

Dr. Edward Stone: None of us knew how long the spacecraft could survive. When I started on the Voyager, my two daughters were young and by the and of course, by the time they were in university, we were already, er, past Saturn. We were on our way to Uranus, they got married. The Voyager just kept going. We had grandchildren and Voyager just kept going and so now our grandchildren are aware of what's happening to Voyager, just like our children were.

Narrator: And what's really amazing is that we're still learning new things from Voyager. Almost 40 years later, Voyager still communicates with this dish over 11 billion miles away. Its message travels at the speed of light, but it still takes more than 17 hours to get here. This little green triangle shows Voyager in deep space. It is a message from the spacecraft. In 2012, Voyager 1 left our solar system and became the first man-made object ever to travel outside the empire of the sun.

8.1

1. When the sun is out, I make sure my son uses sunscreen so he doesn't get sunburnt.
2. Have you read the information about the Red Planet?
3. We are having a picnic, whether it is hot or not. It has been good weather recently, so we are hoping it will be nice.
4. She ate her dinner before she went out at eight o'clock.
5. There are two doctors in the family, and their daughter is also studying medicine.
6. Our guest was in the house for an hour.

8.2

1. The weather is really nice today.
2. I waited for an hour.
3. Are you going there later?
4. I read the book yesterday.
5. We ate our dinner.
6. I don't mind.

8.3

Host: In this episode of *Astronomy Today*, we are looking at space travel and the **journeys** that people hope to make **beyond** the moon. We'll think about the **planets** people haven't visited yet and whether we are likely to visit some of them in the future. Let's begin inside our own solar system, which is made up of all the planets and the sun. Venus, Jupiter and Neptune are probably the first names that come to mind when you think of the solar system. But the planet scientists hope to visit next is Mars. Mars is known as the 'Red Planet' because of its colour. NASA, the US government organization that studies space, so far has only sent robot explorers to Mars. But they are working to send humans to Mars and want to **reach** Mars by the 2030s. Even with the danger, many people want to travel to Mars.

8.4

Host: NASA wants to send humans to an asteroid by 2025. An asteroid is like a very large rock that goes around the sun like the planets do. First, NASA wants to send a robot on a journey to reach the asteroid and take a large boulder from its surface. Once the robot takes the large boulder from the asteroid, the robot will set the boulder on a **path** around the moon. After that, NASA wants to send people to **explore** this asteroid piece in the 2020s. They plan a journey to the boulder in a **spacecraft** named Orion. Orion won't be able to land on the **surface** of Mars, but it will travel to the asteroid boulder to get information. Orion will also help test new spacecraft and give NASA information that it needs to safely send people to Mars.

Outside our solar system, there is a place even more surprising than Mars and many people would go there if we had the spacecraft to send them. Its scientific name is BPM 37093, but it is usually called Lucy. It is actually a dead star or a white dwarf star. It is what is left over when a star uses up all its energy. It doesn't burn anymore, but it shines with heat. But the most surprising fact is that this dead star is a huge diamond. Scientists have always known about the diamond-like white dwarf stars, which are made by heat. They are all outside our own solar system, like Lucy. Lucy is about 4,000 kilometres across, less than half as wide as Earth. Even though it is small, it weighs about as much as our sun. If Lucy were mined, there would be more diamonds found on it than all the diamonds on Earth through history. Even though it is a dead star, this dwarf star is hot. It has a temperature of about 2,700 degrees Celsius. But scientists call Lucy a cold star, because it is only half as hot as our sun. And while the trip to explore Mars is planned for the 2030s, scientists have not found a way to travel outside our own solar system yet. Perhaps one day.

8.5

Host: Hello, everyone. We'll begin today's discussion with a look at how to pay for space exploration. We'll also **evaluate** the benefits of space exploration and whether the money we spend is worth it. We will first look at the **options** for paying for space exploration. I have three **experts** with me today: Dorota Loy, an engineer from the Space Development Project; Raj Padow, a researcher in economics; and Dr Jun Wu, who is a professor of astrophysics. Let me ask Dr Wu to start us off by giving us a little information about the impact of space exploration and the importance of spending money on it.

8.6

Host: Let me ask Dr Wu to start us off by giving us a little information about the impact of space exploration and the importance of spending money on it.

Jun: Thanks for having me. Well, to answer your question, space exploration is important because we do research and get information about many things. For example, as scientists explore space, we learn about biology and about physics, as well as space. So for me, the most important thing is that governments give enough money for future exploration.

Dorota: You have a point that space exploration is used for a lot of scientific study. But it is very expensive and there is less **public** money to pay for it nowadays. Is having the government pay really the only option for paying for space exploration?

Jun: I hear what you're saying, Dorota. It isn't cheap to run space programmes, but the money we spend is certainly worth it. Government and public money must be included. So far, space exploration has shown us many things about how space works, what stars do, the effects on people who stay in space for a long time and so on. We must continue to do this work so that we can explore places in space farther away and ...

Raj: Can I just say something here?

Host: Yes, Raj?

Raj: I agree 100 percent with Dr Wu that we need space exploration. But even he says it is very expensive. I know that we have to spend money to develop our space programmes and we need more money than governments have. So for me, an alternative would be to bring in thinkers from different industries to discuss different ways to pay. If we are exploring space, we could have **private** companies pay for it. For me, this is the main reason we ...

Jun: But Raj, space exploration is so important. Governments must ...

Raj: Sorry, Dr Wu, can I finish my point? If so much money is spent on space exploration, the most important thing should be finding money from places other than the government. It shouldn't be just taxpayers paying for it. Private companies make lots of money from the discoveries made in space exploration, so they should pay for the costs.

Host: Dorota, you haven't said much so far. Any thoughts?

Dorota: Well, I personally don't see a problem. Dr Wu has a good point about public government money and I feel exactly the same as Raj about private money. But we can do both of these things – public or government money, helps us keep the people who know the most, like those at NASA, focused on the research and private money helps bring in other **talent** from companies that would also like to explore space, such as Virgin Galactic or SpaceX. Companies like these have already spent a lot of money on this important type of travel ...

Jun: Yeah, – important space travel that governments should ...

Dorota: Please allow me to finish. There are also other choices that neither of you have talked about yet. Space exploration benefits the world. What about money from private individuals? There are wealthy people around the world that might be interested in giving money for these projects. Also, with the internet, people from around the world could give money for these projects. Lots of people could make donations directly to their favourite projects. I think in the future we can get money for space exploration from more than one place. We should study these different ways and use the best solution.

Host: Dr Wu, Raj Padow, let's get your thoughts on this. Do you agree with these ideas for paying for space exploration?

Jun: Yes ... Dorota could be right. Space exploration needs money to come from many places, as long as the government is still a part of this important area of exploration.

Raj: And I think she might be right, too. But as I said, only if there is money from private companies, too.

Host: OK, so you have some agreement here then. Let's go back to the benefits of space exploration and think about that a little more. So does anybody want to ...

ACKNOWLEDGEMENTS

The authors and publishers acknowledge the following sources of copyright material and are grateful for the permissions granted. While every effort has been made, it has not always been possible to identify the sources of all the material used, or to trace all copyright holders. If any omissions are brought to our notice, we will be happy to include the appropriate acknowledgements on reprinting and in the next update to the digital edition, as applicable.

Key: B = Below, C = Centre, L = Left, R = Right, T = Top.

Photos
All below images are sourced from Getty Images.

pp. 14–15: Barry Kusuma/Photolibrary; p. 19 (a): Danita Delimont/Gallo Images; p. 19 (c): Massimo Pizzotti/Photographer's Choice RF; p. 19 (d): Reza/Hulton Archive; p. 24 (a): Coprid/iStock/Getty Images Plus; p. 24 (b): Malcolm Fife/Photographer's Choice; p. 24 (c): Steve Peterson Photography/Moment; p. 24 (d): kisgorcs/iStock/Getty Images Plus; p. 24 (e): Bruce Bennett/Getty Images News; p. 24 (f): Glow Décor/Glow; p. 24 (g): Ultima_Gaina/iStock/Getty Images Plus; p. 24 (h): zoranm/E+; p. 25: David Nunuk/All Canada Photos; p. 28: Frank Pali/All Canada Photos; p. 32: joe daniel price/Moment; p. 33: Steve Debenport/E+; pp. 36–37: Floris Leeuwenberg/Corbis Documentry; p. 39 (1a): Diana Lee Angstadt/Moment; p. 39 (1b): Dove Lee/Moment; p. 39 (1c): Mimo Khair Photography/Moment; p. 39 (2a): danilovi/E+; p. 39 (2b): skynesher/E+; p. 39 (2c): H. & D. Zielske/LOOK-foto/LOOK; p. 39 (3a): Lindsay Upson/Image Source; p. 39 (3b): Mento/Moment; p. 39 (3c): Keng88Photography/iStock/Getty Images Plus; p. 39 (4a): karandaev/iStock/Getty Images Plus; p. 39 (4b): John Lund/Blend Images; p. 39 (4c): Rogan Macdonald/Cultura; p. 41 (a): Gary Conner/Stockbyte; p. 41 (b): Max Dereta/Photodisc; p. 41 (c): Thomas Lohnes/Getty Images News; p. 46: Brent Winebrenner/Lonely Planet Images; p. 48 (a): Ray Bradshaw/Moment; p. 48 (b): Michael Tham M.H./EyeEm; p. 48 (c): Robert Benson; p. 51 (T): NEZAR BALOUT/AFP; p. 51 (B): Harvey Glen/arabianEye; p. 53: Chris Jackson/Getty Images Entertainment; p. 63 (a): ADRIAN DENNIS/AFP; p. 63 (b): Huntstock; p. 63 (c): Howard Kingsnorth/The Image Bank; p. 63 (d): Kevin Schafer/Photolibrary; p. 63 (e): Pirotehnik/iStock/Getty Images Plus; p. 69: shapecharge/E+; p. 72: Marc Romanelli/Blend Images; pp. 80–81: DeepDesertPhoto/RooM; p. 87: Eric Audras/ONOKY; p. 94 (L): Rolando Gil/The Image Bank; p. 94 (C): Brazil Photos/LightRocket; p. 95: Bill Raften/Photolibrary; pp. 102–103: Peter J Fox/Getty Images Sport; p. 108 (a): Tom Shaw/Getty Images Sport; p. 108 (b): PIERRE VERDY/AFP; p. 108 (c): Power Sport Images/Getty Images Sport; p. 108 (d): Target Presse Agentur Gmbh/Getty Images News; p. 115: Clive Brunskill/Getty Images Sport; p. 120: somnuk krobkum/Moment; pp. 124–125: Bloomberg; p. 138: Hero Images; pp. 146–147: by wildestanimal/Moment Open; p. 151 (a): MileA/iStock/Getty Images Plus; p. 151 (b): Dorling Kindersley; p. 151 (c): T3 Magazine/Future; p. 151 (d): G. Jackson/Arcaid Images; p. 154: Access E/WireImage; p. 160: Access E/WireImage; p. 165: Mondadori Portfolio; pp. 168–169: Neutronman/iStock/Getty Images Plus; p. 175: 7activestudio/iStock/Getty Images; p. 180: NASA/Getty Images News; p. 181: Mark Williamson/Oxford Scientific; p. 182: Digital Vision/Photodisc; p. 186: Bruno Vincent/Getty Images News.

The following images are from other image libraries:
p. 19 (b): Heracles Kritikos/Shutterstock; pp. 58–59: Piero Cruciatti/Alamy Stock Photo; p. 91: Hornbil Images/Alamy Stock Photo; p. 94 (R): Adress Latif/Reuters.

Front cover photography by franckreporter/E+

Video stills
The below stills are sourced from GettyImages.

p. 38: AFP Footage.

The following stills are sourced from other libraries:
p. 16, p. 60, p. 82, p. 104, p. 126, p. 148, p. 170: BBC Worldwide Learning.

Illustrations
p. 99, p. 142: Oxford Designers & Illustrators.

Video
Videos supplied by BBC Worldwide Learning and Getty Images.

ITN; Bob Chappell and John Alfirevich/Image Bank Film; Bloomberg Video – Footage/Bloomberg; Fadil Aziz/DigitalVision; srisadonous/Creatas Video+/Getty Images Plus; AFP Footage; Sky News/Film Image Partner; Barcroft Media – Footage/Barcroft Media Video; Gsmotion/Photolibrary Video; Roberto Machado Noa/LightRocket; Feature Story News – Footage/Getty Images Editorial Footage; Faithfulshot – Footage/Getty Images Editorial Footage; Tribune Broadcasting – Anna Burkart; CrowdSpark; TRAVELXP HD/Image Bank Film; Fraser Hall/Image Bank Film; Manakin/iStock/Getty Images Plus; BBC Worldwide learning.

Corpus
Development of this publication has made use of the Cambridge English Corpus (CEC). The CEC is a multi-billion word computer database of contemporary spoken and written English. It includes British English, American English and other varieties of English. It also includes the Cambridge Learner Corpus, developed in collaboration with the University of Cambridge ESOL Examinations. Cambridge University Press has built up the CEC to provide evidence about language use that helps to produce better language teaching materials.

Cambridge Dictionaries
Cambridge dictionaries are the world's most widely used dictionaries for learners of English. The dictionaries are available in print and online at dictionary.cambridge.org. Copyright © Cambridge University Press, reproduced with permission.

Typeset by emc design ltd.

UNLOCK SECOND EDITION ADVISORY PANEL

We would like to thank the following ELT professionals all around the world for their support, expertise and input throughout the development of *Unlock* Second Edition:

Adnan Abu Ayyash, Birzeit University, Palestine	Takayuki Hara, Kagoshima University, Japan	Megan Putney, Dhofar University, Oman
Bradley Adrain, University of Queensland, Australia	Esengül Hasdemir, Atilim University, Turkey	Wayne Rimmer, United Kingdom
Sarah Ali, Nottingham Trent International College (NTIC), United Kingdom	Irina Idilova, Moscow Institute of Physics and Technology, Russia	Sana Salam, TED University, Turkey
Ana Maria Astiazaran, Colegio Regis La Salle, Mexico	Meena Inguva, Sultan Qaboos University, Oman	Setenay Şekercioglu, Işık University, Turkey
Asmaa Awad, University of Sharjah, United Arab Emirates	Vasilios Konstantinidis, Prince Sultan University, Kingdom of Saudi Arabia	Robert B. Staehlin, Morioka University, Japan
Jesse Balanyk, Zayed University, United Arab Emirates	Andrew Leichsenring, Tamagawa University, Japan	Yizhi Tang, Xueersi English, TAL Group, China
Lenise Butler, Universidad del Valle de México, Mexico	Alexsandra Minic, Modern College of Business and Science, Oman	Valeria Thomson, Muscat College, Oman
Esin Çağlayan, Izmir University of Economics, Turkey	Daniel Newbury, Fuji University, Japan	Amira Traish, University of Sharjah, United Arab Emirates
Matthew Carey, Qatar University, Qatar	Güliz Özgürel, Yaşar University, Turkey	Poh Leng Wendelkin, INTO City, University of London, United Kingdom
Eileen Dickens, Universidad de las Américas, Mexico	Özlem Perks, Istanbul Ticaret University, Turkey	Yoee Yang, The Affiliated High School of SCNU, China
Mireille Bassam Farah, United Arab Emirates	Claudia Piccoli, Harmon Hall, Mexico	Rola Youhia, University of Adelaide College, Australia
Adriana Ghoul, Arab American University, Palestine	Tom Pritchard, University of Edinburgh, United Kingdom	Long Zhao, Xueersi English, TAL Group, China
Burçin Gönülsen, Işık University, Turkey		